THE CRISIS HITS HOME

Stress-Testing Households in
Europe and Central Asia

THE CRISIS HITS HOME

Stress-Testing Households in Europe and Central Asia

Erwin R. Tiongson, Naotaka Sugawara, Victor Sulla,
Ashley Taylor, Anna I. Gueorguieva,
Victoria Levin, and Kalanidhi Subbarao

THE WORLD BANK

Washington, D.C.

ISBN: 978-0-8213-8222-6
e-ISBN: 978-0-8213-8223-3
DOI: 10.1596/978-0-8213-8222-6

Library of Congress Cataloging-in-Publication data has been requested.

Contents

Boxes

Chapter 2

Chapter 3

Figures

Executive Summary

Chapter 1

Chapter 2

Chapter 3

Appendix

Tables

Appendix

Acknowledgments

This report was prepared by a core team led by Erwin R. Tiongson and including (in alphabetical order) Anna I. Gueorguieva, Victoria Levin, Kalanidhi Subbarao, Naotaka Sugawara, Victor Sulla, and Ashley Taylor. The report received generous financial support from the ECA Office of the Chief Economist. This report was undertaken under the guidance of Indermit Gill (Chief Economist), Luca Barbone (Sector Director), Asad Alam (former Sector Manager, currently ECCU3 Country Director), and Benu Bidani (Sector Manager).

The report draws heavily from several background notes and papers including those prepared by Victoria Levin (lessons from previous ECA crises) and Kalanidhi Subbarao (public works programs). It also draws from an ongoing research project conducted by members of the team together with Thorsten Beck and Katie Kibuuka on household indebtedness in Europe and the CIS. The research project is financed by the DECRG Research Support Budget (RF-P115252-RESE-BBRSB). Kechen Chen conducted an initial analysis of the Kazakhstan HBS data in July and August 2008.

The team received valuable comments and suggestions at the concept note, decision draft, and other stages of the preparation process from peer reviewers and numerous colleagues. These include (in alphabetical order) Mohamed Ihsan Ajwad, Emanuele Baldacci (IMF), Lawrence Bouton, R. Sudharshan Canagarajah, Sanjeev Gupta (IMF), Ardo Hansson, Jesko S. Hentschel, Valerie Herzberg, Christos Kostopoulos, Kathy Lindert, Pradeep Mitra, Fernando Montes-Negret, Pierella Paci, Stefano Paternostro, Bryce Quillin, Sophie Sirtaine, and Marijn Verhoeven. Paloma Anos Casero provided many useful suggestions during the early stages of this study. Salman Zaidi offered generous advice at various stages of the preparation process. M. Willem van Eeghen provided valuable guidance in preparing the final version of this report.

A number of individuals generously shared the results of their ongoing empirical analyses and/or their data, including (in alphabetical order) Carlo Azzarri (DECRG), Dániel Holló (Magyar Nemzeti Bank), Kotaro Ishi (IMF), Alejandro Izquierdo (IADB), Sarosh Sattar (ECSPE), Emil Tesliuc (HDNSP), Marijn Verhoeven (PRMPS), Olga Vybornaia (ECSPE), and Alberto Zezza (FAO). This report also draws from many of the ideas first discussed at the World Bank Workshop on Macro Risks and Micro Responses (held in Washington, DC, on February 15, 2008). The team is grateful to the workshop participants, including presenters from the European Bank for Reconstruction and Development, the European Central Bank, the International Monetary Fund, the Center for Strategic Research (Moscow), the National Bank of Poland, and the Economic and Financial Risk Unit of the World Economic Forum.

Abbreviations

ALMP	Active Labor Market Programs
BIS	Bank for International Settlements
CCT	Conditional Cash Transfers
CEMBI	Corporate Emerging Markets Bond Index
CIS	Commonwealth of Independent States
CPI	Consumer Price Index
DECPG	World Bank Development Prospects Group
DECRG	World Bank Development Research Group
EAP	East Asia and the Pacific
EBRD	European Bank for Reconstruction and Development
ECA	Europe and Central Asia
ECB	European Central Bank
ECCU3	World Bank South Caucasus Country Unit
EMBIG	Emerging Markets Bond Index Global
EU	European Union
EU5	Czech Republic, Hungary, Poland, Slovak Republic, and Slovenia
EU8	Member States of the EU (the Czech Republic, Estonia, Hungary, Latvia, Lithuania, Poland, Romania, Slovak Republic)
EU10	New Member States of the EU (Bulgaria, the Czech Republic, Estonia, Hungary, Latvia, Lithuania, Poland, Romania, the Slovak Republic, and Slovenia)
EU-SILC	EU Survey of Income and Living Conditions
FAO	Food and Agriculture Organization
FDI	Foreign direct investment
GDP	Gross domestic product
HBS	Household Budget Survey
HDNSP	Social Protection Team
IADB	Inter-American Development Bank
IMF	International Monetary Fund
LAC	Latin America and the Caribbean
MNB	Magyar Nemzeti Bank (National Bank of Hungary)
MSCI	Morgan Stanley Capital International
NGO	Nongovernmental organization
NPL	National poverty line
OECD	Organisation for Economic Co-operation and Development
PAYG	Pay as you go
PPP	Purchasing power parity
PRMPS	World Bank Public Sector Governance Unit
PUJ	Publicly useful jobs
SPJ	Socially purposeful jobs
WB	World Bank
WEO	World Economic Outlook

Executive Summary

The Europe and Central Asia (ECA) region has been hit by a crisis on multiple fronts. Countries in ECA are facing major, interrelated, external macro-financial shocks. The first is the global growth slowdown leading to falling export market demand. In addition, the prospects for inflows of remittances to low-income countries have been downgraded as economic activity in migrant host countries has declined. The second is the financial deleveraging by major banks and other financial institutions in developed economies, which has markedly reduced the availability, and increased the cost, of external finance across public, corporate, and financial sectors. The third is the recent commodity price changes, which have involved a reversal of much of the commodity price boom of 2007 and 2008. As a result, countries whose exports are focused on commodities have suffered adverse terms of trade pressures, in addition to the quantity shock to export demand. Across countries in the region, unemployment levels have risen while economic activities have collapsed.

The crisis risks reversing the region's recent gains and exposes ECA to significant adverse economic and social impacts. Over the recovery period following the 1998 Russian crisis through 2006, more than 50 million people moved out of poverty in the region. Poverty fell throughout all the sub-regions of ECA, with the middle-income countries of the Commonwealth of Independent States (CIS) experiencing the largest declines in poverty. Poverty reduction in ECA has been driven largely by growth in mean incomes and rising real wages among the working poor. However, the rapidly deteriorating global economic environment is eroding the region's substantial recent gains, and is threatening the welfare of about 160 million people—close to 40 million people who are poor and about 120 million people who are just above the poverty line.

A. Objectives of the Study

The main objective of the study is to understand the impact of these macroeconomic shocks on household well-being. In particular, it seeks to understand the key macroeconomic shocks confronted by the region and the impact of such shocks on household welfare, including the effect on household income flows, consumption levels, and liabilities. It will also assess possible strategies to cope with the crisis and manage the adverse social impact.

The report examines household vulnerabilities along three main transmission channels. Figure 1 represents a stylized diagram for understanding the impact of macroeconomic shocks to date on household welfare. It reflects a summary of the emerging conceptual and empirical understanding of the social effects of macroeconomic crises experienced in various parts of the world over the past three decades. In brief, the diagram focuses on three main channels through which major macroeconomic shocks—such as the regional growth slowdown or the credit crunch—are transmitted to household welfare. These are the income and employment of members of the household; the relative prices of goods and services they purchase; and their access to finance (including the cost of credit and the burden of servicing debt).

The diagram is stylized and abstracts from several important elements. It is simplified and ignores second-round effects and the consequences of multiple shocks, and does not indicate how the social effects are distributed.

Neither does the diagram take into account the role of wealth effects as a transmission channel of the crisis to households, such as via changes in the prices of property, the value of equity holdings (directly or in pension funds), or indeed expectations of future labor income. Changes in wealth may directly lead to adjustments in the consumption behavior of households or indirectly through the role of certain assets, such as property, as collateral that affects a household's ability to access credit. The heterogeneous asset positions of households mean that such wealth changes will lead to redistributions within the household sector, such as between those long or short in a particular asset. Unfortunately, lack of data on household wealth levels and composition precludes detailed stress testing of such wealth effects. However, the build-up of mortgage indebtedness detailed in the report provides some indirect insight into the growing exposure of households' asset positions to property holdings. The above diagram also does not address the role of government policy (including fiscal and monetary) and social assistance (though social assistance may be thought of as a source of income). Government policy can, in fact, either mitigate shocks or exacerbate them, depending on how it is formulated and implemented. A further transmission channel of the real and financial impacts of the crisis through to household welfare, though not explicitly addressed, is

FIGURE 1

Macroeconomic Shocks and Household Welfare: Stylized Transmission Channels

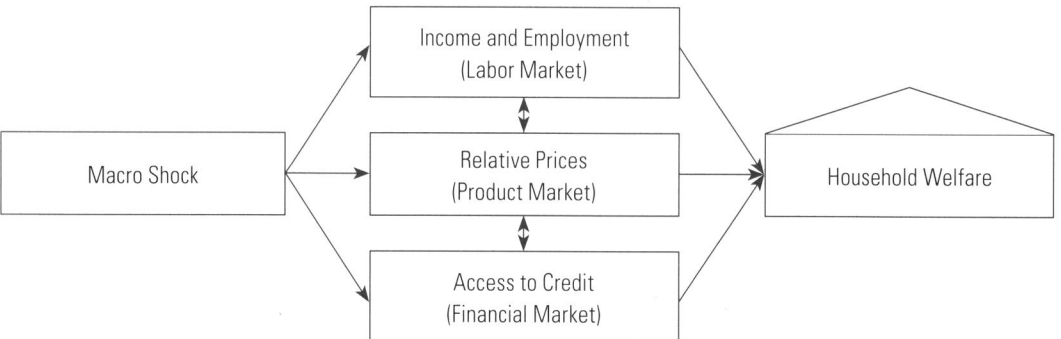

pension provision. The nature and magnitude of the effects of the crisis via this channel depend crucially on the structure of the pension system, in particular the mix between pay-as-you-go, funded, and voluntary pension systems.

The report analyzes household vulnerabilities by examining credit markets, external prices (food and fuel), and income shocks to date and by assessing their impact on household welfare. Because actual household survey data over the crisis period will typically not be available for some time to come, we use the most recent pre-crisis household data along with aggregate macroeconomic outturns to simulate the impact on households of key economic shocks already taking place. The impact on household well-being is quantified as the change in the household debt service burden, the fall in real income, or movements into poverty, as appropriate. The report presents regional overviews along with cross-country comparisons and contrasts. It also presents selected country examples, depending on data availability and relevant economic developments, to illustrate the incidence and distribution of specific vulnerabilities within countries.

The microeconomic simulation in the report draws on a large, cross-country database of household surveys. The report brings together for the first time comparable cross-country data on household indebtedness for a large group of ECA countries using the European Union Survey of Income and Living Conditions and Household Budget Surveys. The report also highlights newly updated information on household consumption from the ECA Household Data Archives. Comparisons with Western Europe and other advanced economies are also used to inform the analysis when relevant data are available.

B.   Main Findings

The results of the analysis suggest that the adverse effects of the crisis on households—via credit market shocks, food/fuel price shocks, and income shocks—are widespread. Both poor households and nonpoor households are vulnerable depending on the economic shock, the specific transmission channel, and selected household characteristics.

FIGURE 2
Household Debt in ECA, 2008
In percent of GDP

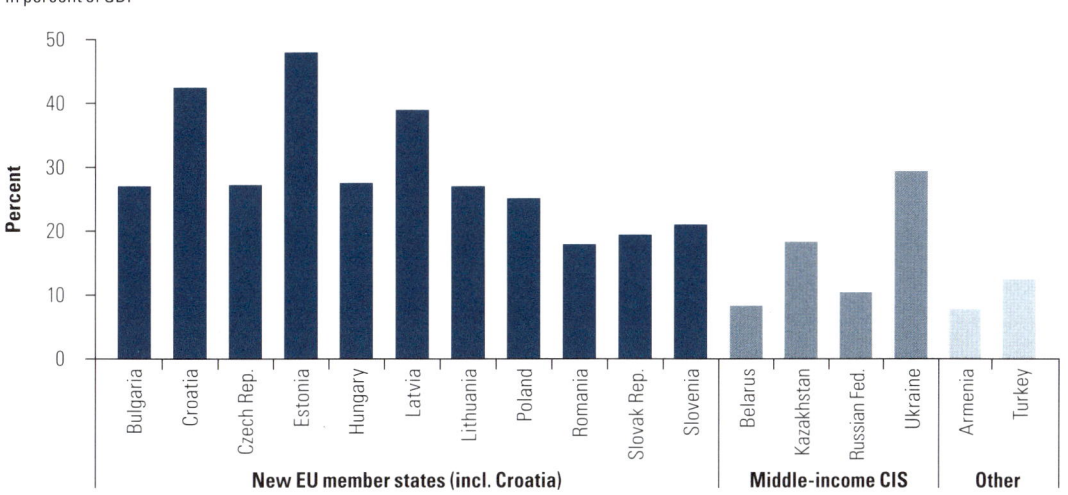

Credit Market Shocks

The rapid rise in household indebtedness—in the new EU member states as well as in some Western Balkan countries, such as Albania and Serbia, and CIS countries such as Ukraine—has exposed households to a number of credit market shocks. There is no doubt that household debt holding has improved the lives of many, allowing them to smooth consumption and share risks, purchase durables, and invest in housing stock. At the same time, the nature of household debt in ECA is such that households are now facing exchange rate and interest rate shocks, with few opportunities for hedging and with little prior knowledge of their vulnerability.

Within countries, household indebtedness is more common than previously understood. Mortgage loans, in particular, have grown rapidly in recent years among poorer and middle-income households in a number of EU10 countries. Both poor households and nonpoor households are exposed to the risks of unsustainable debt service burdens.

The results of stress tests on household indebtedness in selected countries suggest that ongoing macroeconomic shocks may significantly expand the pool of households that will be unable to meet debt service obligations. Interest rate shocks in Estonia, Lithuania, and Hungary, for example, increase the share of vulnerable households or borrowers at risk (in percent of all indebted households) by up to 20 percentage points, depending on the magnitude and severity of the shock. Unemployment and exchange rate shocks also expand the share of vulnerable households (out of all indebted households) by several percentage points. Many of those household borrowers at risk of unsustainable debt burdens are from the richer income quintiles. Although the shares of indebted households and households at risk in the ECA region still lag behind those of richer countries, the aggregate effects of rising debt service burdens are already being seen in rising household loan delinquency rates, as unemployment has increased.

External Price Shocks

The food and fuel crisis may not be over. Food and fuel prices have abated worldwide because of the worsening global financial crisis—the economic recession or slowdown in many countries across regions—and, as a result, global demand for commodities has fallen. In addition, increased agriculture production activity

FIGURE 3

The Share of Vulnerable Households Before and After an Unemployment Shock

In percent of indebted households

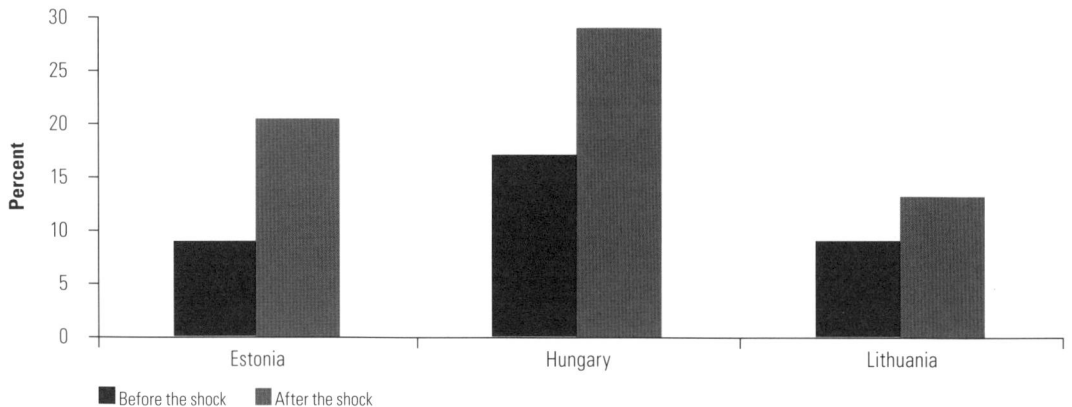

FIGURE 4

Kyrgyz Republic: Poverty and the Food Price Crisis

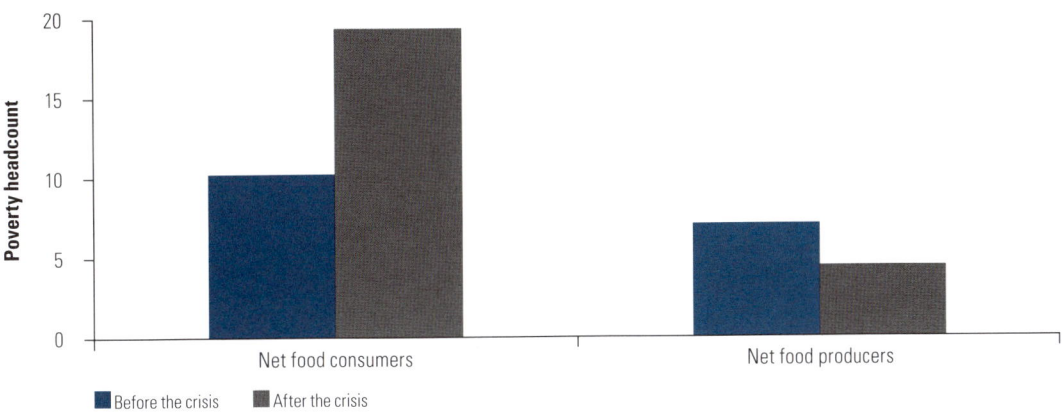

led to a bountiful 2008 harvest and eased global commodity shortages. However, international commodity price levels have not returned to pre-2007 levels. Specialists have also pointed to longer-term challenges in global food production that are yet to be addressed. In addition, falling currencies in some EU10 countries are resulting in a new round of price increases, depending on the share of imported food and fuel in local consumption and the degree of pass-through of exchange rate changes in domestic prices. Finally, in a number of countries such as Belarus, Moldova, and Ukraine, the utility reform program remains largely incomplete. As a result, for reasons of economic efficiency or fiscal consolidation, a number of countries will have to adjust their tariffs to cost-recovery levels in the coming years.

There is significant heterogeneity within countries in the welfare impact of commodity price shocks. The net effect of a food price shock depends on whether households are net producers or net consumers of food, it depends on their intensity of food consumption and the availability of cheaper substitutes, and it depends on their livelihood strategies, access to agriculture assets and inputs, and their ability to take advantage of profitable opportunities in agriculture. These multiple considerations suggest that, at least in principle, the poor are not necessarily the hardest hit. However, the food share of total household consumption typically falls with income; in some of the low-income countries in the region, the food share of consumption among the poor is 70 to 80 percent. Moreover, in reality, the poor are the worst hit, as many of the poor in Albania, Kyrgyz Republic, and Tajikistan, for example, are also observed to be net consumers, with limited access to agricultural assets and inputs.

Income Shocks

Poverty will rise. Simulations suggest that by 2010, there will be 11 million *more* people in poverty, and *more* than 23 million more people will find themselves just above ECA's international poverty line, relative to baseline pre-crisis projections. The growth in poverty would represent a fifth of the ECA population who moved out of poverty between 1998 and 2006. This is not surprising given that poverty in ECA is shallow, characterized by large numbers of individuals susceptible to falling into poverty even with modest falls in average income. Alternatively, one could think of them as the recent-poor, with tenuous links to the labor market, with little precautionary savings, and

FIGURE 5

The Poor and Vulnerable Population, 2007–10

Using the $5-a-day measure of poverty

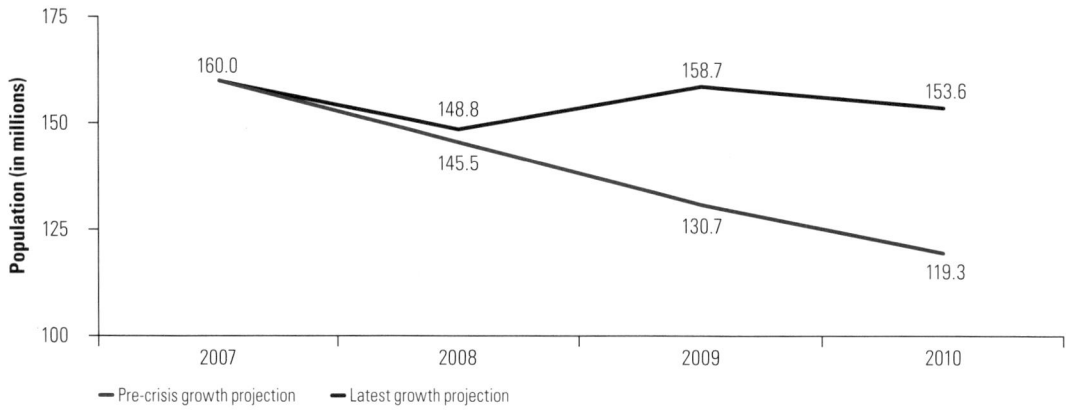

— Pre-crisis growth projection   — Latest growth projection

who are likely to have benefited from recent credit and construction booms.

The magnitude of the poverty impact varies by sub-regions. The middle-income CIS countries, on average, have seen the largest and most significant downward revisions to their gross domestic product growth projections. As a result, and by construction, they are also seeing the largest percentage point increases in the projected poverty headcount. They are followed closely by the low-income CIS.

The aggregate results mask the heterogeneity of impact within countries, including the concentration of the poverty impact in selected economic sectors. Country studies recently completed suggest that for economic shocks transmitted primarily through the labor market, poverty will rise especially among households that have been dependent on remittance inflows and those previously employed in booming construction sectors where economic activity is now projected to decline sharply.

The results of the analysis are indicative of how vulnerabilities are distributed across countries and, within countries, across broad types of households. In some ways, the estimated effects may be understated because they capture only some of the first-round

effects. On the other hand, general equilibrium effects will either dampen or worsen some of these effects.

The second-order effects on human capital accumulation and social capital will be significant. Lessons from the region's own experiences suggest that transitory shocks' long-term toll on human capital has been substantial because families curbed their education and health investments in response to a banking or exchange rate crisis. Crises may lead to increased social unrest, criminal activity, and human trafficking; disrupt communal and ethnic relations; or bring down fragile governments and fledgling democracies.

Coping with the Crisis

Compared to previous crises, the scope for households to engage in their traditional coping strategies may be more limited. During previous crises, households found secondary employment, relied on transfers from friends and families, or left for work abroad to augment family income. Because of the global nature of the crisis, and because macroeconomic shocks are hitting households on multiple fronts, many of these coping strategies are no longer viable. For the poorest households, subsistence farming may still be feasible, though evidence from the recent food price shock suggests that many of the poorest households do not have access to agricultural assets and inputs. For some, transitions into informal sector employment may be possible, though for many households, earnings from informal sector activity will be insufficient to offset the poverty impact of the crisis.

Policy Responses

Fiscal policy responses in the short term are constrained by rapidly falling revenues. Substantial government deficits are currently projected for the region. It would be essential to determine the overall fiscal adjustment warranted for macroeconomic stability and debt sustainability, taking into account initial conditions and the likely impact of the crisis on public finances. Economies that experienced strong initial fiscal and external positions are likely to have more room for expansionary fiscal policy and can afford a fiscal stimulus package, while those with weaker initial positions may require substantial fiscal adjustment. Where there are no new official or alternative sources of financing and little scope exists to mobilize revenues, some countries will likely resort to across-the-board cuts in spending. Although social safety nets will be among those items likely to be cut as revenues fall, protecting these programs—and possibly expanding some of them, where some reallocation of resources is possible—will be an important element in the response to the crisis.

Inappropriate policy responses to economic shocks may have welfare consequences far larger than the welfare losses resulting directly from the shocks themselves. In 2007–08, some countries imposed trade restrictions and price controls in response to rising food prices. Such policies redistribute income away from rural food producers (who tend to be poorer) to urban consumers (who tend to be richer). The net social

impact may be even larger when considering the impact of such policies on production incentives and the likely spillover impacts of restrictive trade policies on neighboring countries, thus exacerbating regional welfare consequences.

The region's social assistance systems vary in size and targeting performance, and not every program can and should be scaled up. In addition, some of these programs will have to be cut as revenues fall. The response to the crisis will vary across countries and may include, among other things, expanding some well-performing programs and reforming relatively less effective interventions. Some of those who will fall into poverty because of the crisis—the "new poor"—may not be easily reached by existing social protection programs. For example, returning migrants do not qualify for unemployment insurance.

The ECA region should consider new instruments of social protection. Social safety nets in ECA need to be strengthened to handle the challenges of global and domestic risks. The experiences of other countries suggest that programs such as workfare and public works programs can be appropriate instruments for protecting the vulnerable from immediate as well as longer-term (second-round) consequences of transitory shocks on nonincome dimensions of welfare, including human capital accumulation. There are a few, albeit limited, country experiences with workfare in ECA—in Bulgaria, Poland, the Slovak Republic, and Slovenia. Some insights from these country experiences can inform the broader application of workfare in ECA so that they can be efficient instruments for social risk mitigation while minimizing displacement effects.

The prioritization of labor-intensive public investments could be an important response to the crisis while creating the conditions for medium-term growth. Such a strategy can create employment opportunities, as in workfare and public works programs, while creating the infrastructure that supports economic recovery and economic growth in the medium term.

Longer-Term Policy Responses

Over the longer term, there are various measures for limiting the risks borne by households as financial markets deepen. On the demand side, promoting financial literacy may help households to understand the risks they expose themselves to because of their consumption, employment, or borrowing choices. In addition, a whole host of macro-financial policies, such as prudential norms as adopted by some EU10 countries to limit foreign currency exposures of households, can be used in combination to help mitigate the potential risks associated with increased exposures of households to credit and financial markets.

It is important that policy responses do not conflict with the key longer-term reform agenda. For example, authorities should guard against reversal of efforts to lower quasi-fiscal deficits in the energy sector, which is an ongoing challenge in many ECA countries, and they should maintain an open and transparent trading regime. Some countries in ECA adopted restrictive trade and price controls in response to the food price increases in 2007 but many of them have now been reversed.

Diversified sources of economic growth will be critical in helping dampen ECA countries' vulnerability to macroeconomic shocks. In some countries in ECA, recent growth performance has been underpinned by economic activity concentrated in a few sectors, such as the housing or construction sector, or income flows from some dominant source, such as migrant labor.

Monitoring systems are important. Guaranteeing that statistical monitoring systems are in place and that relevant household data are collected regularly and made available for analysis are important measures for ensuring that household vulnerabilities to a range of potential shocks are understood in a timely manner and that those households at risk can be reached by a country's social protection system.

The resilience of households to macroeconomic shocks ultimately depends upon the economy's institutional readiness, the flexibility of the economic policy regime, and the ability of the population to adjust. Policy and institutional preparedness is essential so that countries can manage the adverse social impacts of macroeconomic shocks. This requires ex ante analysis of risks, a good understanding of their possible transmission channels if triggered, and their possible impacts on households; developing approaches that ensure that the state does not intervene excessively in terms of detrimental longer-term distortions to incentives or fiscal sustainability; and having a comprehensive social safety net system that provides for countercyclical and scalable interventions.

CHAPTER 1

Macroeconomic Shocks

A. Introduction

The Europe and Central Asia (ECA) region has been hit by a crisis on multiple fronts. The first is the global growth slowdown leading to falling export market demand. In addition, the prospects for inflows of remittances to low-income countries have been downgraded as economic activity in migrant host countries has declined. The second is the financial deleveraging by major banks and other financial institutions in developed economies, which has markedly reduced the availability, and increased the cost, of external finance across public, corporate, and financial sectors. The third is the recent commodity price changes, which have involved a reversal of much of the commodity price boom of 2007 and 2008.

This chapter examines how the external shocks arising from the global economic crisis can be transmitted through to macro shocks affecting the welfare of households, via their income, access to credit, wealth, and relative prices of food and fuel. Section B first introduces a simple stylized framework of the transmission channels, which provides the structure for the subsequent discussion. Section C examines the external shocks and their transmission channels to countries within the region. The nature and extent of the transmission of these shocks through to households depend crucially on an economy's macroeconomic strengths and vulnerabilities, such as the degree of international integration, the strength of sectoral balance sheets, and domestic policy stance, which are discussed in Section D. Finally, Section E outlines the main resulting macro shocks to household welfare, the micro implications of which are analyzed in subsequent chapters.

B. Macro Shocks and Household Welfare: Framework

Major macroeconomic shocks are transmitted through to household welfare via various mechanisms; this report focuses on three

FIGURE 1.1

Macroeconomic Shocks and Household Welfare: Stylized Transmission Channels

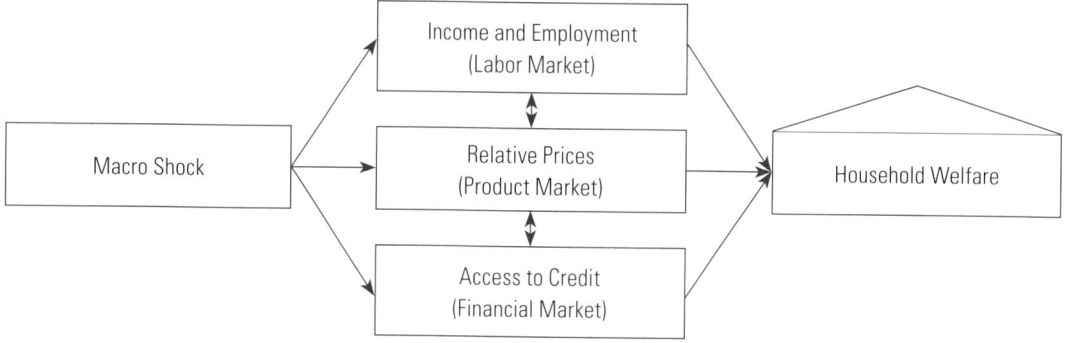

main channels. Figure 1.1 represents a highly stylized diagram for understanding the impact of macroeconomic shocks on household welfare. It reflects a summary of the emerging conceptual and empirical understanding of the social effects of macroeconomic crises experienced in various parts of the world over the past three decades. The main channels considered are the income and employment of members of the household; the relative prices of goods and services they purchase; and their access to financial market (including the cost of credit and the burden of servicing debt). As discussed below, in the current context the shocks to household welfare via these channels have arisen primarily because of the impact of external shocks, such as to global income, credit conditions, and commodity prices, whose effects depend crucially on the domestic economy's macro strengths and vulnerabilities.

The diagram is stylized and abstracts from a few important elements. It ignores second-round effects (such as on human capital accumulation, access to social services, and disruptions to communal ties) and the consequences of jointly occurring crises and, as drafted, does not indicate how the social effects are distributed (along geographic, occupational, sectoral, gender, or income lines), though all these will be considered in varying degrees

below. Neither does the diagram take into account the role of wealth effects as a transmission channel of the crisis to households, such as via changes in the prices of property, the value of equity holdings (directly or in pension funds), or indeed expectations of future labor income. Changes in wealth may directly lead to adjustment in the consumption behavior of individual households or may do so indirectly via the role of certain assets, such as property, as collateral that affects their ability to access credit. The heterogeneous asset positions of households mean that such wealth changes are likely to lead to redistributions within the household sector, such as between those long or short in a particular asset. Unfortunately, lack of data on household wealth levels and composition precludes detailed stress testing of such wealth effects. However, the build-up of mortgage indebtedness detailed in the report provides some indirect insight into the growing exposure of households' asset positions to property holdings. The above diagram also does not address the role of government policy (including fiscal and monetary) and social assistance (though social assistance may be thought of as a source of income). Government policies can, in fact, either mitigate shocks or exacerbate them, depending on how they are formulated and implemented.

C. External Shocks and Transmission Channels[1]

Global Income

Since 2006, the growth of the major developed economy countries, and world export demand, has weakened as the global credit crisis, which began in the summer of 2007, unfolded. The IMF's April 2009 World Economic Outlook projected a contraction in world growth of 1.3 percent in 2009 with growth recovering to 1.9 percent in 2010 (figure 1.2). These shocks to global income may be transmitted to countries within the region via trade flows and remittances. Demand for exports from the region

FIGURE 1.2

Global Growth and Trade Slowdown
Annual real growth

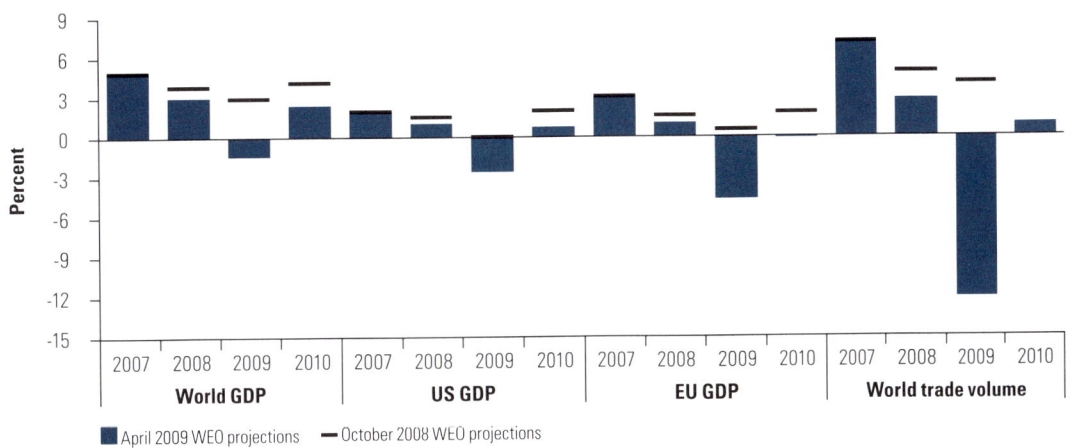

Source: IMF WEO October 2008 and April 2009.
Note: 2009 and 2010 are projections.
Trade defined as volume of goods and services.

FIGURE 1.3

Export and Import Growth
Growth year-on-year

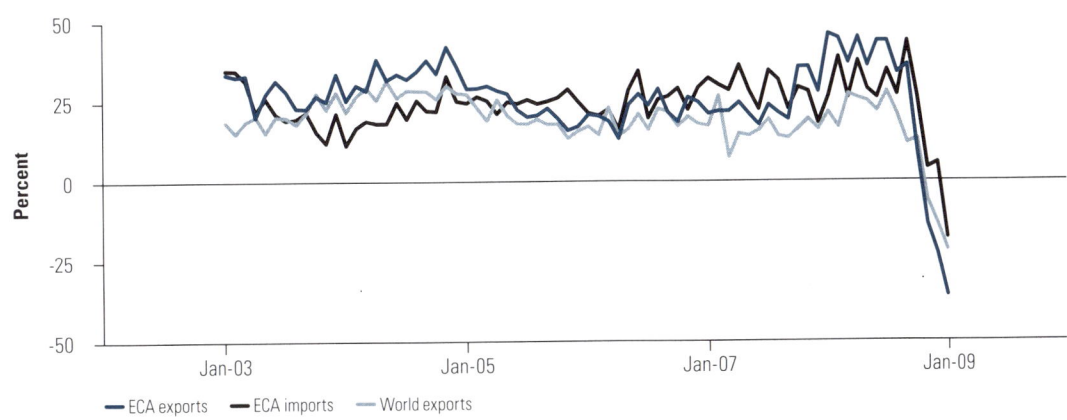

Source: WB DECPG and staff calculations.
Note: Change in US dollar seasonally adjusted values.

has fallen sharply, with the GDP of advanced economies projected to contract by 3.8 percent in 2009. At the same time, the credit crunch is also impeding the ability to finance export trade credits. As a result, the World Bank's 2009 Global Economic Prospects predicts that world trade will decline in 2009 for the first time since 1982 (with the IMF April 2009 WEO projecting an 11 percent contraction in the volume of world trade in goods and services in 2009). The impact of these trends on trade for ECA countries has resulted in a precipitous drop in export and import values (figure 1.3). As discussed in more detail later, remittances have already fallen sharply in some countries and prospects for 2009 inflows of remittances to developing countries have been downgraded as economic activity in migrant host countries has declined. For many countries in ECA, particularly those in the former Soviet Union, this reflects the impact of the slowdown in Russia and the valuation effects of the nominal depreciation of the ruble, that is, a second-round regional shock, rather than being directly due to the slow-down in developed markets.

Global Credit Conditions

As the financial crisis deepened from September 2008, mounting concerns over liquidity risk, asset quality, and counterparty credit risk and enhanced risk aversion have resulted in significant deleveraging and attempts to reduce portfolio risk by financial institutions. This has not only affected the ability of financial institutions and corporates in developed economies to obtain financing but also led to a retrenchment of the international exposures of banks and, for many countries, a sharp reduction in their ability to access international finance. Gross capital flows to emerging and developing economies have fallen significantly (figure 1.4). The contraction, which has been across asset classes, has been particularly marked for ECA (whose share of such flows fell from around 40 percent in 2007 and 2008 to just over 20 percent in 2009). In terms of international banking exposures, after peaking at end-March 2008, the consolidated foreign claims of Bank for International Settlements (BIS) creditor banks, in real terms, on Organization for Economic Co-operation and Development (OECD) economies fell by around 20 percent

FIGURE 1.4
Gross Capital Flows to Emerging and Developing Economies

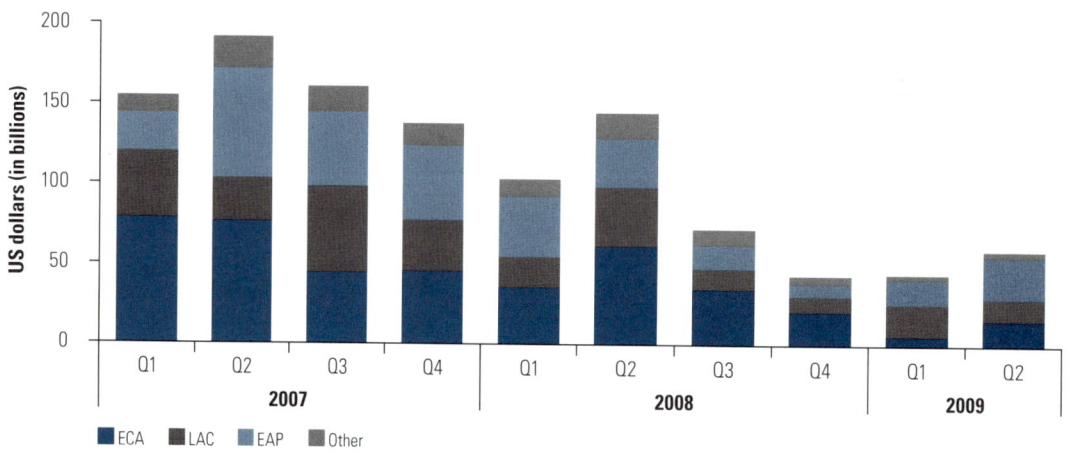

Source: DECPG.
Note: US dollar values deflated by US CPI. 2009 Q1 data are preliminary estimates.

FIGURE 1.5
Contraction in BIS Creditor Bank Foreign Claims
In Q1 2009 prices

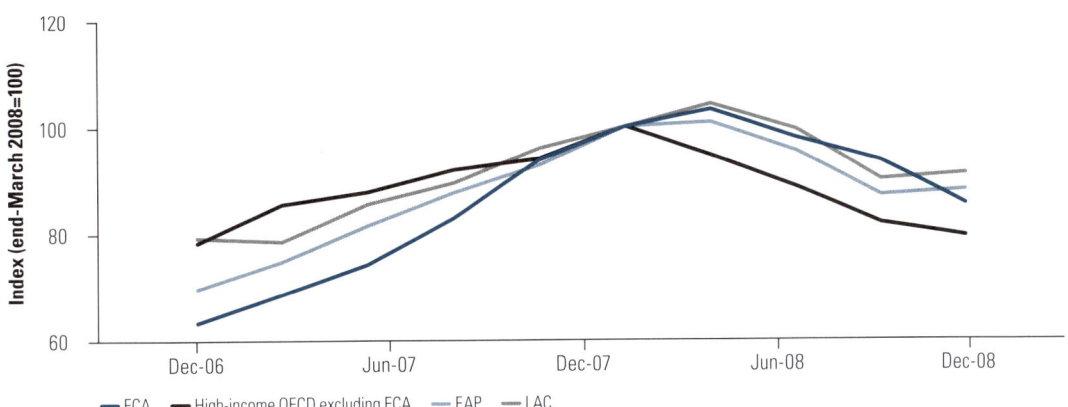

Sources: BIS, IMF International Financial Statistics and staff calculations.

to end-March 2009 (figure 1.5). Real BIS creditor banks' foreign claims on emerging economies generally peaked at end-June 2008 and by end-March 2009 had fallen by 17 percent for ECA compared with around 12.5 percent for Latin America and the Caribbean and East Asia and Pacific.

Regional equity and exchange rates came under pressure during late 2008 as foreign investors drew back funds from the region, and concerns over the domestic impact of the financial crisis mounted. Despite somewhat of a reversal in recent months, the downturn in financial markets in ECA since early 2008, and since September 2008 in particular, has been widespread and deep across asset classes and countries. These declines unwound a large part of the gains made in equity and sovereign bond valuations during the asset price run-up of preceding years (in which the average dollar value of the Morgan Stanley Capital International [MSCI] Emerging Europe equity index increased by over seven times from October 2001 to December 2007). The reduced demand for emerging market assets also contributed to marked local currency nominal depreciations as discussed in detail below. Secondary market

credit spreads also increased substantially. The JP Morgan Emerging Markets Bond Index Global (EMBIG) Emerging Europe sovereign spread increased from 275 basis points on 1 September 2008 to over 900 basis points in late October. Having declined to 740 basis points by end-2008, the spread continued to narrow through 2009, with the average monthly spread reaching around 400 basis points in July 2009. Similarly, the cost of credit default protection via credit default swaps and external corporate funding rates increased sharply. For example, the JP Morgan Corporate Emerging Markets Bond Index (CEMBI) external corporate spread for emerging Europe (covering Kazakhstan, Russia, and Ukraine) increased from 530 basis points to 1,560 basis points at end-2008 before declining to an average of around 730 basis points in July 2009. In addition to the falls in bond and equity markets, interbank markets exhibited rising spreads in October and November reflecting international funding pressures and domestic liquidity concerns.

Global Commodity Prices
The global growth slowdown has contributed to a sharp easing in global food, fuel,

FIGURE 1.6
Commodity Price Developments

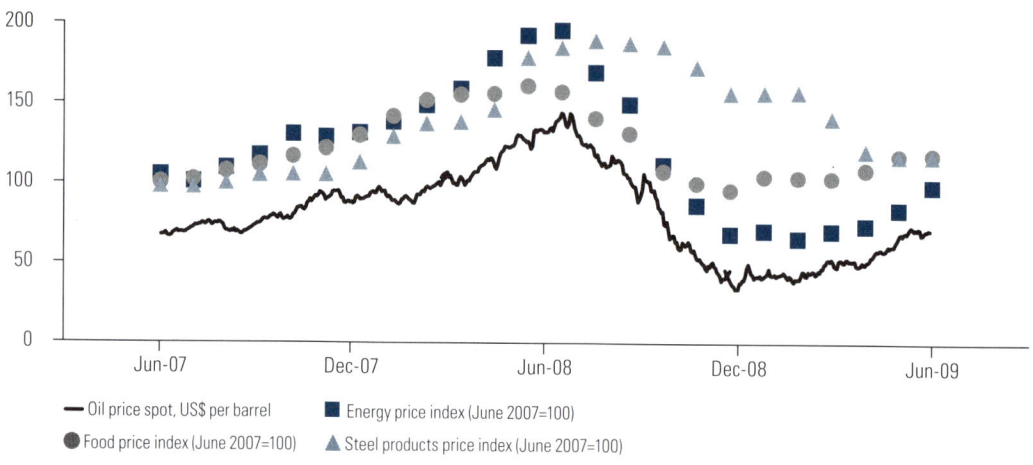

Source: WB DECPG and staff calculations.
Note: Oil price is a simple average of Brent, West Texas Intermediate, and Dubai crude oil prices.

and other commodity prices since mid-2008. Although making projections is particularly difficult given the current macro-financial uncertainty, the June 2009 World Bank Global Development Finance forecasts a 43 percent fall in the US dollar oil price in 2009 relative to 2008, with a rise of 13 percent in 2010. Non-oil commodity prices are projected to fall by 30 percent in 2009 with a further 2 percent decline in 2010. In recent months, there has been some recovery in prices of some commodities, such as oil (figure 1.6). Clearly, the overall impact of these price movements on a country's external payment position is dependent upon its net consumption mix and respective export and import price elasticities. Countries whose exports are focused on commodities have thus suffered adverse terms of trade pressures, in addition to the quantity shock to export demand. For example, while the weakening oil price has had material implications on external and fiscal positions in Russia and Kazakhstan, the downturn in steel prices adversely affected the external outlook for countries such as Ukraine with the rapid

fall in fertilizer prices having similar impact in economies such as Belarus.

D.   Context: Macroeconomic Strengths and Vulnerabilities

The impact on a country's economic outlook of the above external shocks depends upon its potential exposure, which can be mapped through different stages of the transmission mechanism. The first is the extent of international integration of the country via trade and financial channels (including remittances). The second is the structure and health of sectoral balance sheets, such as in terms of external financing requirements, currency, and maturity mismatches. The third stage is the ability of policymakers to mitigate the impact of the shock through the policy stance in terms of monetary policy, exchange rate flexibility, and, linked to the strength of public sector balance sheets, the current fiscal stance and the ability to use fiscal policy measures to absorb the impact of the global shocks.

International Integration

The increasing international integration of countries in ECA over the past decade via trade, income, and capital flows has enabled countries to benefit from the growth and financing of partners but also provides increasing channels through which global and regional shocks are transmitted to domestic economies. Over the past decade, the ratio of the total US dollar value of merchandise trade (exports plus imports) of countries in ECA to their gross domestic product (GDP) has increased from around 45 percent in 1998 to 57 percent in 2007. This follows the general growth in global trade over this period. However, there are marked variations in the level of trade openness across sub-regions in ECA. For example, over this period the merchandise trade for the new European Union (EU) member states in Central Europe and the Baltics (the EU8) rose from 70 percent to 107 percent while for middle-income CIS the ratio was broadly flat over this period.

In addition to the variation in the level of trade openness within the region, there are considerable differences in the patterns of trade partners and major trading products across sub-regions, as would be expected from gravity-type models of trade flows. The importance of the EU as an export market, and hence the exposure of countries to the contraction in demand from the EU as a result of the crisis, is particularly marked in the EU members of ECA, Southeastern Europe, and Turkey. The extent of intra-regional trade linkages within ECA is particularly high between the middle- and lower-income Commonwealth of Independent States (CIS) countries. In terms of major product categories, the exports of these two groups of countries are highly concentrated in petroleum and petroleum products (around 44 and 53 percent of total exports in 2007, respectively), whose international prices have dropped from their mid-2008 highs. Iron and steel export earnings

in the former sub-region and Southeastern Europe are also vulnerable to the commodity price and activity downturns (accounting for just under 10 percent of exports in both cases). Trade patterns in the EU8 are strongly intra-industry and particularly focused on consumer durables including products such as road vehicles (around 15 percent of exports and 10 percent of imports) and electrical and telecom equipment which again are subject to strong demand shocks as consumption falls in partner regions.

Net capital flows to the region doubled as a proportion of GDP from 2002 to 2007, financing consumption and investment while increasing the impact of any sudden stops to such flows. From a level of around 4 percent of GDP in 2002–2004, net capital flows to ECA increased to around 8 percent of GDP in 2007 buoyed by factors including the global search-for-yield, the EU accession process, and foreign direct investment (FDI) related to commodity investments. This broad pattern of growth in relative flows was present across sub-regions. The mean level of net capital flows to GDP across countries reached over 15 percent in Southeastern Europe and over 10 percent in the EU8. Although the mean level fell in low-income CIS countries, this reflected net capital outflows from Azerbaijan.

Increased cross-border lending and foreign bank ownership have both contributed to the sharp rise in international banking claims on ECA. The level of gross international assets of BIS creditor banks in ECA, on a locational basis, rose from around 13 percent of GDP at end-2004 to 21 percent of GDP at end-2007. There are considerable variations across sub-regions with the CIS countries having net claims on BIS creditor banks for most of the period from 2003. In contrast, the net assets of BIS creditor banks on the Baltics reached over 70 percent of GDP in early 2008 (up from 30 percent in mid-2005) with levels of around 40 percent of GDP on the EU5 and Southeastern

Europe. These figures compare to net assets of BIS creditor banks on the five Asian crisis countries (Indonesia, Korea, Malaysia, Philippines, and Thailand) of around 20 percent of GDP in mid-2007.

The rise in consolidated foreign claims of BIS creditor banks (i.e., netting out intra-group exposures) in recent years has been particularly marked in ECA's EU member states and Southeastern Europe, increasing the potential for two-way spillovers between local and Western European banking systems. Foreign claims on ECA, which include international claims (i.e., cross-border claims plus local claims of foreign affiliates in foreign currency) and local claims of foreign affiliates in local currency, peaked at around 45 percent of GDP at end-June 2008, up from around 30 percent in the two years from June 2008, before falling to around 35 percent of GDP by end-2008. In 2008, foreign claims on the Baltic countries peaked at almost 140 percent of GDP, Southeastern Europe at over 100 percent, and the EU5 at over 80 percent of GDP. Much of this increase has been due to the growth in local claims of western European foreign affiliates. The level of foreign claims to GDP on the EU8 and Southeastern European countries at end-2008 remains considerably higher than the averages for OECD countries and indeed that observed for the Asian-crisis countries at end-1997. International claims tend to be concentrated on the non-bank private sector and banking sectors rather than the public sector with the share of short-term international claims relatively high in Turkey and the middle-income CIS countries. The geographic patterns of banking sector interlinkages via foreign claims have evolved in a different manner across sub-regions. While all regions have seen a relative reduction in the share of German banks in their foreign claims, Swedish banks are the primary foreign claim creditor in the Baltics and the share of Austrian claims has risen in the Central European new member states of the EU, the middle-income CIS, and Southeastern Europe.

Remittance inflows have grown rapidly over the past five years and for lower-income economies in ECA outweigh the intra- and extra-regional financial inter-linkages via private capital flows. The dollar value of remittance inflows to ECA grew at an annualized growth rate of around 37 percent between 2003 and 2007 versus around 19 percent per annum for developing countries as a whole. Of those countries with high inflows of remittances relative to GDP, annualized growth rates of remittance inflows of 32 percent were seen for Moldova, 66 percent for Azerbaijan, 74 percent for the Kyrgyz Republic, and 84 percent for Tajikistan. In such countries, the level of external financial inflows from remittances far exceeds that of capital inflows, exposing countries to reductions in employment and wages in migrant host countries more than direct exposures to developments in international financial markets. For example, in Tajikistan and Moldova in 2007 it is estimated that remittance inflows to GDP were around 46 percent and 34 percent respectively compared with net capital inflows of around 10 percent of GDP.

For many countries, particularly in the lower-income CIS, the exposures to recent external shocks come particularly via their second-round regional impact, for example in terms of remittances and trade flows with Russia. For ECA's EU member states and Southeastern Europe, financial, particularly banking, and trade integration developments highlighted the increasing interdependences with economic developments in Western Europe and global financial conditions. However, the patterns of trade and importance of remittances for lower-income CIS focus attention on the potential for intra-regional spillovers arising from developments in Russia. For example, exports to Russia accounted for around 35 percent of Belarus' exports in 2007 (or roughly 20 percent of GDP) and around a quarter of the exports of Kyrgyz Republic, Moldova, Ukraine, and Uzbekistan. Similarly, in 2007 flows from Russia accounted for almost all the remittance inflows for the highly remittance-dependent economies of Kyrgyz Republic and Tajikistan and over half the remittances to Moldova. As Russia's economy grew strongly between 2003 and 2007 (with annual GDP growth in the range of 6.4 to 8 percent), these inter-linkages led to strong positive spillovers to partner countries. The flipside is the exposure of these countries to any downturn in Russia (with the World Bank's June 2009 Russian Economic Report forecasting a real GDP contraction of 7.9 percent in 2009 with growth of 2.5 percent in 2010).

Balance Sheet Strengths and Weaknesses

The composition and strengths of domestic sectoral balance sheets are crucial determinants of the impact on the economy of external shocks transmitted via the various international inter-linkages discussed above. Of particular interest in ECA have been the interrelated developments in household and financial sector balance sheets over the past five years relating to increasing household indebtedness and their exposures to currency and interest rate shocks.

Household indebtedness has grown rapidly in many ECA countries. Between 2002 and 2007, for example, household debt relative to GDP grew at an annual average rate of 37 percent in the newer member countries of the EU, while rising only by 7 percent in the older EU member countries. In the new EU members, household debt now represents a little over a quarter of GDP, although it remains below the 65 percent level in older EU members. Household indebtedness also has been growing rapidly in a number of countries in the CIS countries and the Western Balkans. The rising trends in household indebtedness, and the associated risks and benefits, are analyzed in more detail in chapter 2.

The growth in household indebtedness follows the rapid expansion in credit to the private sector more generally.[2] Buoyant housing markets, favorable macroeconomic and financial conditions, and the increasing availability of a broad range of mortgage instruments have underpinned it. For the new EU member countries, it has also been suggested that the convergence in living standards toward the EU average has helped accelerate credit growth.[3] Over this same period, household financial assets also grew rapidly, though not at the same pace as household indebtedness. As a result, the net financial assets relative to GDP of the household sector have fallen in many countries in the past few years, although on a per capita basis net financial assets have generally risen since 2000 with some decline in recent years because of the pace of accumulation of liabilities. To the extent that the rises in household liabilities are associated with mortgages, they are likely to be matched by greater property assets, although unfortunately data on the overall balance sheet positions of the household sector, including both financial and non-financial assets such as property, are not available.

The rise in the gross financial positions of the household sector, and their changing composition, has both brought benefits and introduced new sectoral vulnerabilities. As household financial positions have grown, there has been a shift toward housing loans or mortgages on the liability side of the balance sheet and an increasing share of equities and pension and mutual funds on the asset side. On the one hand, rising indebtedness reflects the benefits of financial sector development, allowing households to smooth their consumption over time and acquire home ownership without significant savings. Changes in the asset side of the balance sheet brought increasing diversification and exposure to higher yielding asset classes than the traditional deposits and currency. On the other hand, these developments bring the potential for greater exposures of households' net financial positions to currency, asset pricing, and interest rate risks. (This will be discussed in greater depth in the next chapter.) If the respective risks are not hedged and they subsequently materialize, they may lead to deteriorations in households' ability to service their debt obligations. This in turn can adversely affect the health of financial sector balance sheets with second-round implications for households in terms of the availability and cost of credit.

Banking sector balance sheets in ECA have expanded rapidly in the past five years, particularly in the Baltics and middle-income CIS countries, funded increasingly by external parent groups and wholesale markets. Credit growth has covered both the household sector and non-bank private corporate sector. As a result, the mean private credit to GDP of countries in ECA roughly doubled from 2003 to 40 percent in 2007 (with the median ratio rising from 19 to 33 percent). In the Baltics, the mean level of private credit to GDP tripled over this period to 71 percent with the means for the middle- and low-income CIS groupings doubling to around 40 and 18 percent respectively. These levels compare to means of 120 percent, 48 percent, and 33 percent for OECD countries, middle-income, and low-income developing country sub-samples respectively.

Average bank credit-to-deposit ratios had reached around 120 percent in ECA by 2007, leading to concern over funding and liquidity risks. The growth in credit to GDP in general through 2002 to 2007 has been associated with rising credit-to-deposit ratios, that is, increased reliance on non-deposit funding sources. However, both trends have been particularly marked in countries within ECA. Some of these non-deposit funds reflect increased access to parental funding sources, as the trend toward increased foreign ownership of banking sectors in ECA has continued in recent years or, in the case of many of ECA's EU member states, stabilized at high levels. Foreign operations have been attracted by relatively high returns within ECA in comparison to developed banking markets, at least up to 2007. Some of the major parent banks in the region themselves also appeared vulnerable to liquidity and funding risks (e.g.,

with net loans to consumer and short-term funding as of end-2007 in the range of 100 to 150 percent). The high level of intra-regional linkages through the set of major parent banks raised concerns over the impact of group liquidity problems on local banking systems and the related regulatory coordination issues.

Although the banking system-level picture going into late 2008 from standard asset quality and capital adequacy indicators revealed only a limited number of weaker outliers, such lagged aggregate indicators may not provide an accurate picture of the current health of banking sectors. For example, national poverty line (NPL) ratios may be relatively low because of the recent rapid expansion of credit more than offsetting reclassification of loans as problematic. In addition, rising interest rates on their own can cause a deterioration of capital adequacy ratios in a mark-to-market environment. Furthermore, a more general weakening of asset quality may increase solvency concerns, rather than the proximate liquidity concerns of late 2008, in less robust banking sectors.

As is well known, many of the economies in ECA, particularly in the Baltics and central Europe, entered 2008 with substantial current account deficits. Much of the funding for these has come from the international bank flows that are projected to decline markedly in 2009. Even those countries more reliant on FDI financing are likely to face increasing difficulties in funding given the general downturn in growth prospects in the region and corporate sector difficulties in developed economies. In some of the cases of previous notable reversals current account deficits, such as in the Asian crisis, adjustment via the trade balance was possible because of a relatively supportive external environment which unfortunately is not the case for the current deficits in the ECA region.

Policy Stance

The ability of policy measures to either support domestic balance sheets in the face of external shocks or mitigate the transmission of these shocks to the household sector is constrained by initial conditions in terms of fiscal space, exchange rate arrangements, and inflationary outlook. Indeed the nature of the balance sheet strengths and weaknesses also guides the potential policy responses to the external shocks. For example, a relatively weak banking sector with high levels of foreign liabilities may limit the overall impact of exchange rate depreciation on economic activity given the scope for adverse balance sheet effects to offset, or outweigh, any positive benefits in external trade positions. Such considerations may caution against significant exchange rate loosening.

On the fiscal side, the ability of economies to use government spending to address the adverse income shock is generally constrained (or nonexistent) in the presence of large and harder to finance current account deficits. In some cases, it may also be limited through debt sustainability concerns arising from structural deficits and possible contingent liabilities arising from banking sector recapitalizations. Although oil exporters, such as Russia and Kazakhstan, entered this period with stronger external and fiscal reserves than did other ECA countries, their scope to employ these funds has become more limited in the face of falling oil prices. While reduced demand and lower commodity prices have reduced overheating pressures in certain countries, inflationary concerns remain in a number of countries during the pass-through of exchange rate depreciation. In other countries, the presence of fixed exchange rate regimes limits the usage of monetary policy to respond to external shocks. Political considerations, of course, add a further complexity to these policy trade-offs.

E. Shocks to Household Welfare

Depending on the strengths and weaknesses in macro vulnerabilities, and policy responses, the global shocks may result in a range of shocks to household consumption and welfare. The next chapters examine the potential impact of shocks to household income via credit market shocks, external prices (food and fuel), and income shocks. The macro context of each of these shocks is outlined below, in addition to a brief discussion of the potential for wealth effects, which, as mentioned above, are not included in the subsequent microanalysis for data availability reasons.

Income Shocks

Shocks to household income arising from the economic crisis may arise through a variety of channels and, depending on the household, may be viewed as temporary or permanent. First, labor income may fall as a result of the loss of employment or falling real wages for those who remain in work. Second, declining remittance inflows are another channel through which household income may fall. Finally, changes in social protection policies as a result of the crisis may also affect household incomes.

Though the exposures to external shocks and strengths of initial balance sheets and policy stances vary across countries, there has been a broad-based reduction in real activity in ECA as a result of the global economic and financial crisis. After turning negative in July 2008, the 3-month on 3-month growth in industrial production in ECA contracted at an increasingly rapid rate from October 2008, reaching around –40 percent on an annualized rate in January 2009. The severity of this downturn has exceeded even the contraction in the OECD countries. The scale of the real slowdown is also evident in the magnitude of the GDP contractions in 2009. For example, Ukraine suffered a 20 percent year-on-year real GDP contraction in Q1 2009 with contractions in the Baltics in the range of 12 to 19 percent in Q1 and 17 to 23 percent in Q2 (according to preliminary estimates.

As real activity has fallen, there is also increasing evidence of the transmission of

FIGURE 1.7

Sharp Contractions in Industrial Production

Percent change 3 month on 3 month, seasonally adjusted annualized rate

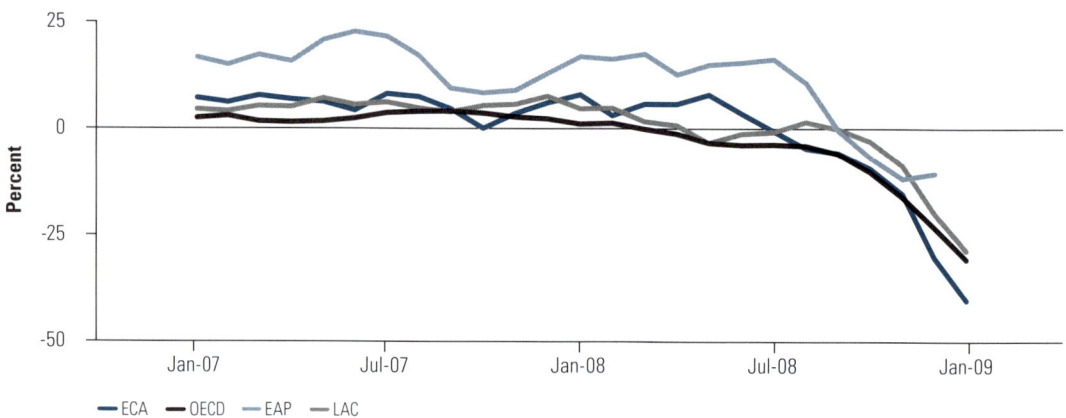

Source: WB DECPG.

FIGURE 1.8

Rising Unemployment Rates

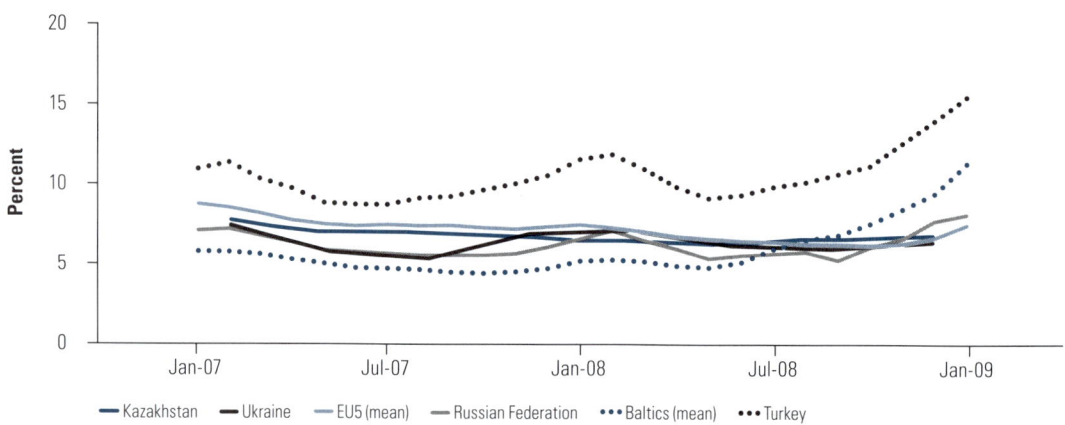

Sources: UN Economic Commission for Europe, Turkish Statistical Institute, the Agency of Statistics of the Republic of Kazakhstan.
Notes: Unemployment rates based on labor force surveys. Break in Turkey series methodology at January 2008.

the crisis through to rising unemployment numbers and declining real wage growth. Unemployment rates have been gradually increasing since mid-2008. The Baltic countries, where Latvia and Estonia experienced GDP contractions in 2008, have shown the earliest and particularly steep rises in unemployment but rates have also started to show an upward trend in many other countries across the region. Real wage growth has also turned downward in a number of countries. For example, real wages in Ukraine fell by 12 percent year-on-year in Q1 2009 compared with growth of around 13 percent in Q1 2008.

Remittance inflows have also taken a sharp downturn, tracking developments in the major sources of funds, in particular Russia and the EU. Slower global and regional growth lowers demand for migrant workers from ECA. For example, growth in the Russian construction sector, an important source of employment for regional migrants, has decelerated sharply. As credit conditions tighten further, construction sector activity is likely to continue to decline. Indeed, formal remittance outflows from Russia to CIS countries contracted by 31 percent year-on-year in US dollar terms in Q1 2009 compared with growth of 12 percent in Q4 2008. This compares to depreciation of the average ruble to US dollar exchange rate of 29 percent year-on-year in Q1 and 10 percent in Q4. Formal remittance inflows, in US dollars, for Tajikistan fell 36 percent year-on-year in the first five months of 2009 with inflows to Georgia and Moldova also down 21 percent and 32 percent year-on-year respectively in the first half of 2009, tracking declines in Russian construction activity. After annual growth of around 37 percent per year from 2004 through 2007, the growth

FIGURE 1.9

Sharp Deceleration in Formal Remittance Inflows

Growth in 3 month moving average, percent year-on-year

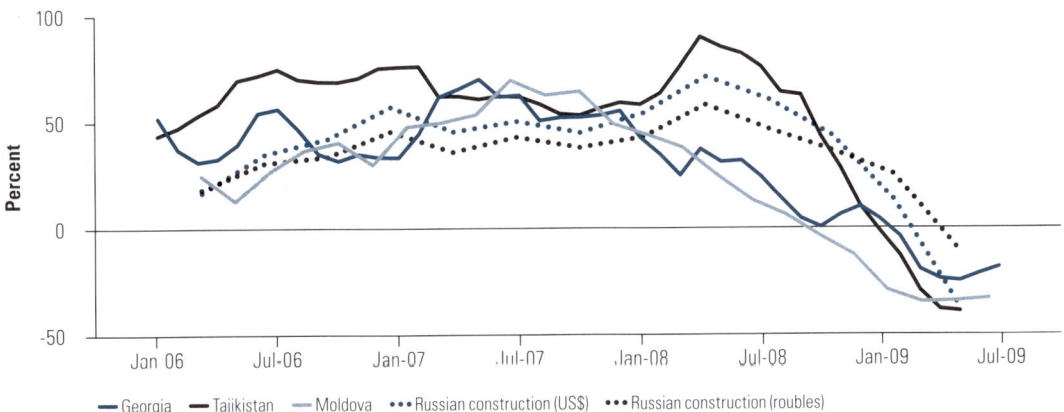

Sources: National authorities, IMF International Financial Statistics, Datastream, and staff calculations.

Notes: Remittances are from money transfer data. Russian construction is the value of works performed in current prices and is converted from Russian rubles into US dollars at the average exchange rate of period.

FIGURE 1.10

Growth in Remittance Inflows

Nominal US dollar

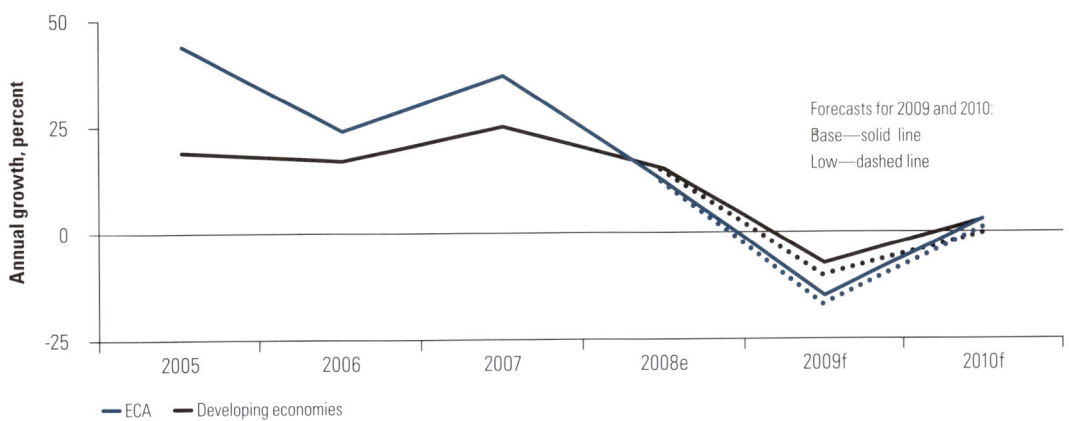

Sources: WB DECPG Migration and Development Brief, 13 July 2009.

in the nominal dollar value of inward remittances to the region is estimated by the World Bank to have declined to around 12 percent in 2008 with a contraction of 15 to 17 percent forecast for 2009. This is roughly double the projected baseline contraction for total remittances to developing countries and compares to a contraction of 16 percent in 1999 during the Russian crisis period. These effects will be particularly felt in selected countries in Southeastern Europe and the low-income CIS where remittances are the largest source of external finance and constitute large portions of GDP.

Looking forward, the likely magnitude and timing of these adverse income shocks is dependent upon the growth outlook for the region. This outlook has been subject to continual, and significant, downgrades from October 2008. As forecasts have been downgraded, the uncertainty around them (as reflected in the variation in the forecasts of contributors) has increased. Official growth projections of the International Monetary Fund (IMF) and World Bank have been continually revised since October in response to the changing national and global economic conditions. The IMF's

April 2009 World Economic Outlook (WEO) forecasts are for a contraction of over 10 percent in the Baltics in 2009, around 6 percent in the middle-income CIS countries, and 5 percent in Turkey. Combined with contractions of around 2 to 3 percent forecast for Southeastern Europe and the Central European new member states and some positive growth in the low-income CIS, the overall contraction in GDP in ECA in 2009 is forecast to be just over 4 percent with a recovery to 1 percent growth in 2010. Of particular interest, in terms of the potential drivers of economic recovery, is the global nature of the downturn with the contraction in developed economies limiting the scope for export-led recoveries, as pursued, for example, in the Asian crisis countries.

The quality of economic recovery also matters. In addition to substantial uncertainty regarding the duration and severity of the crisis, it is unclear whether economic growth—if and when the recovery begins—will necessarily translate fully into growth in household consumption. In part, the poverty impact of economic recovery depends on whether renewed growth is accompanied by, for example, commensurate increases in wage, employment

FIGURE 1.11

Growth around Recent Crisis Periods: 1997–98 and 2008–09
Real GDP growth

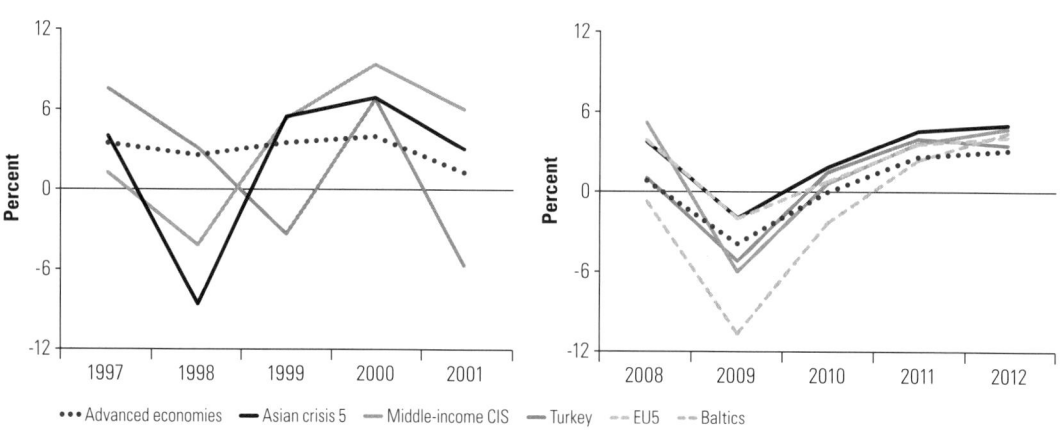

Source: IMF WEO (April 2009) database and staff calculations.
Note: Regional averages are weighted using country shares in global PPP GDP.

FIGURE 1.12

"Credit-less Growth" in Emerging Markets and in the U.S. Great Depression

Emerging markets **U.S. Great Depression**

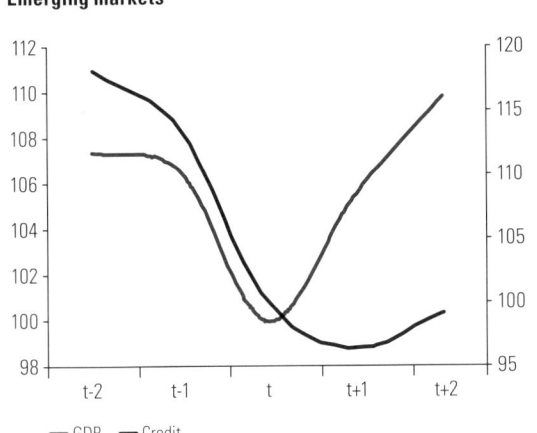

— GDP — Credit

Source: Calvo, Izquierdo, and Talvi 2006a.

expansion, and renewed availability of credit for households and enterprises. Some recent research, the implications of which are yet to be fully explored, suggests substantial heterogeneity in countries' experience of the resumption of economic growth following a systemic financial crisis.

In the recovery period following the 1998 Russia crisis, some ECA countries experienced what has come to be known as "jobless growth." In part, this may have been due to rapid wage increases that outstripped productivity gains, thus constraining job creation and squeezing profits in the process. Not surprisingly, poverty has been least responsive in countries where employment creation has been limited and where jobless men and women account for a significant share of the poor.[4] Along with modest economic growth and stalled poverty reduction (in some cases, rising poverty), these countries have also experienced rising inequality.

The experience of systemic financial crises in emerging markets—including a number of ECA countries—also suggests the possibility of economic recovery without credit. The first set of results from recent pioneering research, in what has been incorporated into

the international finance lexicon as "credit-less growth," indicates that economic output may recover without any measurable recovery in domestic or external credit.[5] These studies have also documented comparable developments in the United States following the Great Depression. Researchers speculate that this phenomenon may be driven in part by enterprises postponing their investment projects or, where investments have been observed to increase, by financing new investment projects out of earnings or funds from informal credit sources. Because these types of economic recovery have just been recently documented, the household welfare implications of such experiences have not yet been explored. One possibility would be that private consumption may grow more slowly (compared with consumption growth following other types of recession), as households restore their overleveraged balance sheets and increase their precautionary savings.[6]

It is not clear whether the ECA region is likely to experience such "credit-less growth" when the region recovers. It has been suggested that credit-less growth was made possible in the past in countries such as Argentina mostly because of rapid export growth. As mentioned, a major difference with the emerging market crises of the late 1980s is the global nature of the crisis, which effectively rules out an export-led recovery heavily reliant on growth in developed markets.[7]

Credit Market Shocks

Funding pressures and rising credit risks within domestic banking sectors have resulted in a general tightening of domestic credit conditions for households and the private sector more generally. On the quantity side, many countries in ECA have seen a rapid deceleration in the expansion of domestic credit, reflecting the drying up of external funding and concerns over potential credit risks. In some countries, such as Ukraine, the level of nominal private credit outstanding has remained flat or declined in the first half of 2009, with real credit now declining. On the cost of financing, the wide variety of household interest rates, by currency and maturity, makes it difficult to provide a comprehensive assessment of changes in lending rates. However, there was a gradual rise in rates on euro housing loans through 2008. Since October/November 2008, the euro rates

have dropped off, as policy rate and quantitative easing have been adopted, and also likely demand has dropped. However, of course, these euro rates do not reflect the burden of mortgage repayments in local currency, which increased markedly with the depreciations during the fall of 2008. Ukraine's average US dollar exchange rate in July 2009 remained depreciated by 40 percent compared with its level at the beginning of September 2008, with Poland and Hungary depreciating by 22 percent and 13 percent, respectively, against the euro over the same period. Some countries, such as Belarus and Kazakhstan, have undertaken step devaluations of their currencies (although the fixed exchange rate regimes in countries such as the Baltics and Bulgaria have remained firm).

External Price Shocks

Food and fuel prices rose sharply in many ECA countries in 2007 and through the first three quarters of 2008. Between 2006 and 2008, global food and fuel inflation doubled. The rapid increase in food prices was underpinned by significant droughts in various parts of the world including in some countries in

FIGURE 1.13
Local Currency Depreciations
In US dollars per local currency

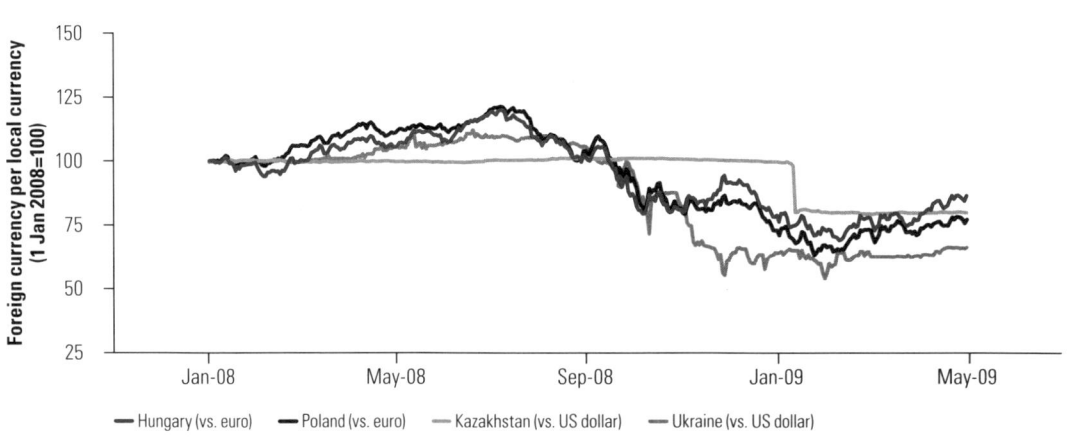

Sources: Datastream and staff calculations.

the ECA region, shifts toward bio-fuel production, declining inventories and tight commodity market conditions, and rising demand in emerging markets. Over this same period, energy prices reached record highs. A number of countries in the region were particularly hard hit, including Kazakhstan, the Kyrgyz Republic, and Tajikistan. In many of the CIS countries, inflation rose close to 20 percent in 2008.

As discussed above, as the global financial crisis has worsened, food and fuel prices have abated worldwide. In large part, this has been driven by the worsening global financial crisis, the economic recession in many countries across different regions and the economic slowdown, more generally, and, as a result, falling global demand for commodities. In addition, the increased agriculture production activity, following soaring food prices and higher returns to agricultural activity, led to a bountiful 2008 harvest, easing global commodity shortages.

For many countries in ECA, however, there are reasons to believe that the impact of the adverse impact of the food and fuel crisis on households may not be over. The rationale for this view can be split into near- and medium-term factors. In the near term, the significant depreciations of local currencies as detailed above serve as offsetting factors against the decline in the US dollar international prices (see figure 1.14). In addition, some have expressed concern that inflation risks may persist with the continuing pass-through of recent food and fuel price increases, due to lags in shipping and distribution.[8] There is also some indication that falling global commodity prices have not translated into lower retail food prices locally in these economies, in part because hedge contracts may have previously locked in higher prices.[9] In addition, while price levels may have come down, they could still be at levels substantially higher than their pre-2007 or pre-2008 levels. The marked fall in international food prices in US dollar terms from late 2008 has not been reflected in a number of food price Consumer Price Index (CPI) sub-indices (figure 1.15). Indeed, these sub-indices have continued to rise over this period in a number of countries.

FIGURE 1.14

International Food and Energy Price Movements and Local Currency Equivalent Indices

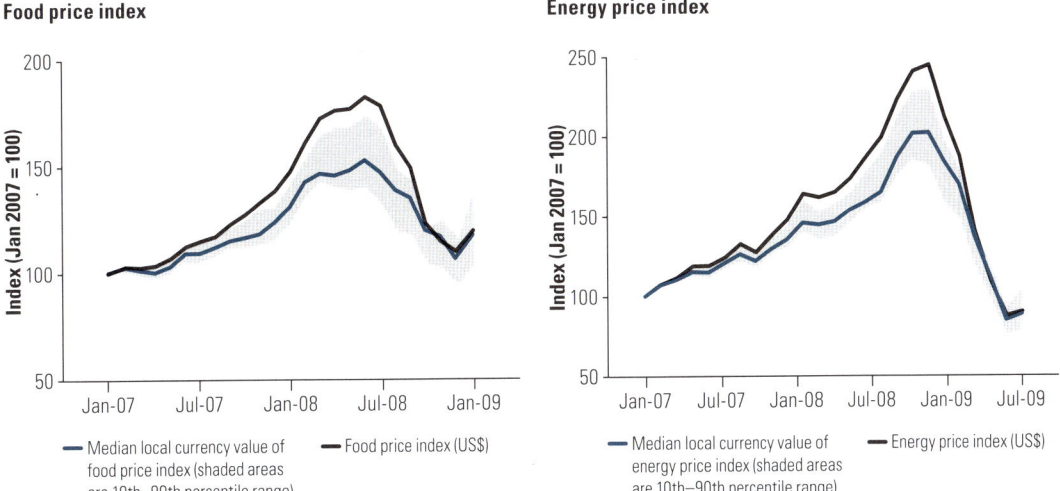

Sources: Eurostat, State Statistics Committee of Ukraine, DECPG.

Notes: US dollar indices converted into local currency value using monthly average exchange rates.

FIGURE 1.15
CPI Food Price Sub-indices: Selected Countries

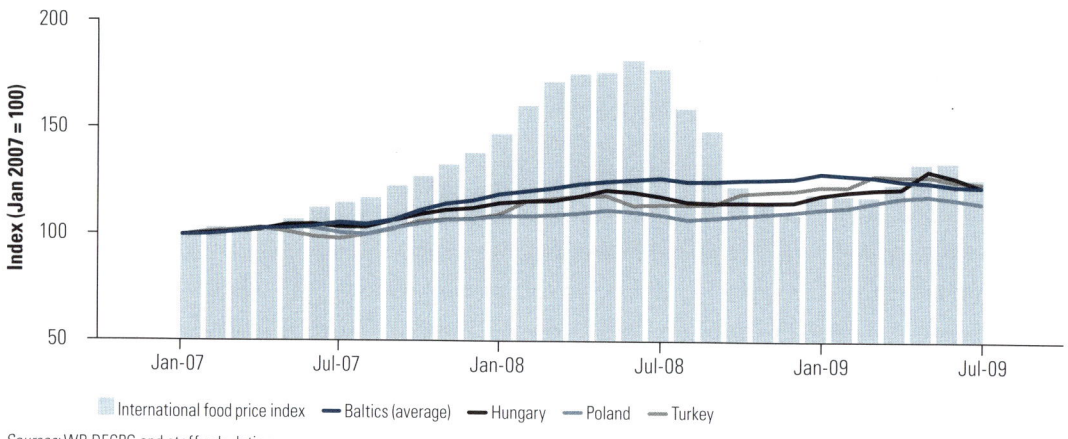

Sources: WB DECPG and staff calculations.

FIGURE 1.16
Local Currency Equity Market Declines across ECA

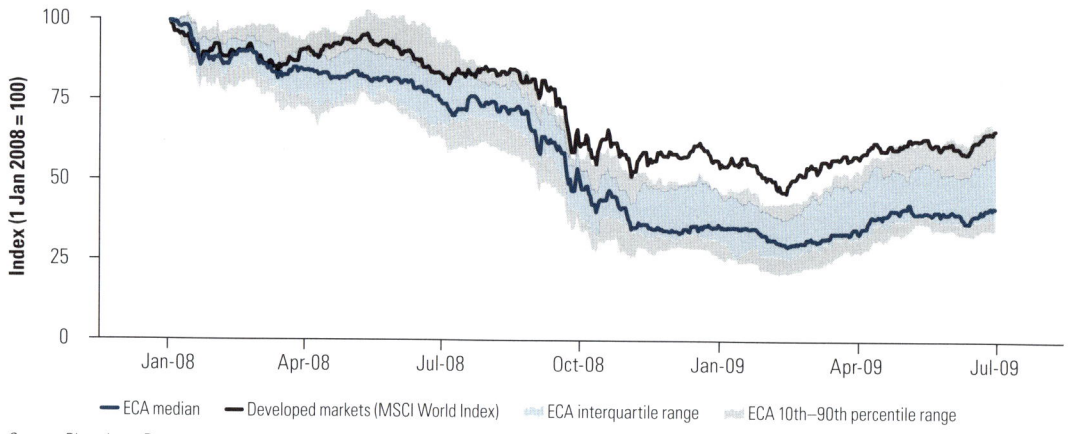

Sources: Bloomberg, Datastream, and staff calculations.

In some CIS countries, there are also prospects for further rounds of external energy price shocks in the near term as Russia moves toward full market pricing for its energy exports. The price of imported natural gas faced by consumers in Moldova, for example, is still below European market prices and is expected to converge to European levels in the near future. In Ukraine, some have argued that energy networks have been historically underfunded and

energy tariffs will have to rise to ensure these networks' financial viability.[10] In the Western Balkans, increasing tariffs to cost-recovery levels will be an important component of electricity sector reform.

As the global recession worsens, it may undercut both public and private investments in the agriculture sector, thus curbing agricultural production. The results of some simulations conducted at the International Food

FIGURE 1.17
Housing Prices in Selected ECA Countries
Growth year-on-year

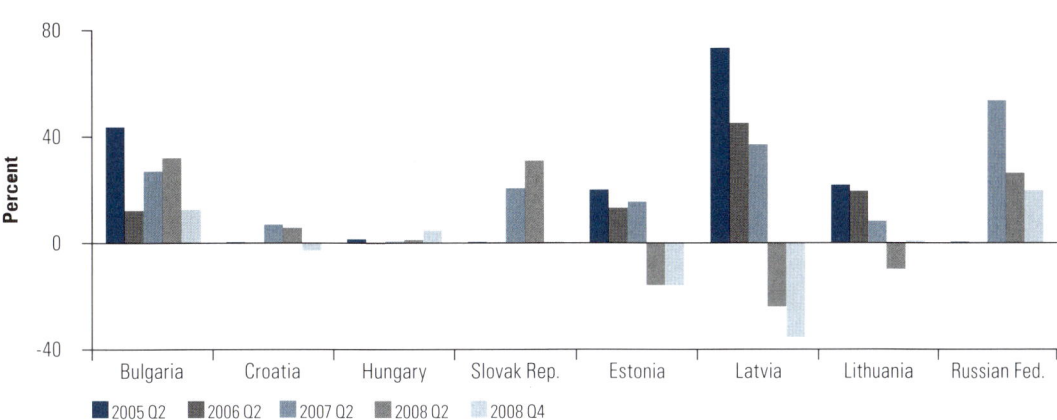

Source: Knight Frank Global House Price Index, various issues.

Policy Research Institute suggest that a global economic recession that depresses agricultural investment can be associated with cereal prices that are 30 percent higher over the longer term than in the absence of a recession.[11]

Wealth Shocks

Households who were long in equities and property or short in foreign currency were particularly exposed to the shocks to hit their net worth position over the past six months. For example, the median fall in local equity indices from 1 January 2008 through to their July 2009 average levels was 60 percent, with a 40 percent median fall alone over the two months from 1 September 2008. These compare with falls of 38 percent and 25 percent respectively for the MSCI developed equities index in local currencies. As discussed above, households' financial assets in the form of mutual fund and pension fund holdings have increased in recent years in many countries in ECA, along with their holdings of residential property. However, it is unclear to what extent the reduction in asset values through the downturn in asset prices (or increase in the local currency value of liabilities denominated in foreign currencies)

has, or will, lead to a significant wealth effect on consumption. There have also been major changes in the path of house prices in recent years in many ECA countries, as in developed markets. For example, in Estonia and Latvia house prices fell in Q4 2008 by around 16 percent and 36 percent year-on-year respectively compared with growth rates reaching roughly 20 percent and 60 percent in Q1 2007. Such price changes lead to redistributions of wealth between those long or short in housing stocks. These can then affect the distribution of consumption via direct wealth effects and via the impacts of changing collateral values on credit constraints. Indeed, household-level analysis in the United Kingdom has found the largest elasticity of consumption with respect to housing prices in older homeowners with an insignificant elasticity for younger renters.[12]

A further transmission channel of the real and financial impacts of the crisis through to household welfare is via pension provision. The nature and magnitude of the effects of the crisis via this channel depend crucially on the structure of the pension system, in particular the mix between pay-as-you-go (PAYG), funded, and voluntary pension systems.[13] For example, the main transmission channel for public PAYG systems is via the impact of the crisis on contributions, through rising unemployment and potentially reduced wage growth. Funded pension systems are exposed to declining asset values (particularly affecting those individuals reaching retirement age during the crisis). Voluntary pensions may also suffer strong adverse effects via this channel, particularly via the wider equity exposures of defined contribution funds, or through the impact of declining corporate health on the defined benefit schemes.

Almost all countries in ECA, except for Kosovo and Kazakhstan, have some form of PAYG system, helping mitigate the direct pension impact of the crisis. However, the ability of countries to absorb rising pension deficits as a result of falling contributions is dependent upon their fiscal space. Indeed, in some countries that have been particularly affected by the crisis, revisions to state pension provision may form part of the fiscal adjustment. In Latvia, for example, significant pension cuts have been recently proposed.

Those countries, which adopted fully funded defined-contribution schemes as an integral part of their mandatory pension schemes, appear most directly vulnerable to the crisis. This group includes thirteen countries in ECA, mainly EU members but also Croatia, Macedonia, Kosovo, Kazakhstan, and Russia. However, in these countries the near-term implications of the fall in asset prices for households in aggregate may be limited for a number of reasons. First, with the exception of Kosovo and Kazakhstan, where 100 percent of contributions are in the funded pillar, these countries place a heavy weight on public provision (with 6.7 percent to 35 percent of contributions in the funded pillar). Second, in the near term relatively few workers are retiring with direct exposure to such second-tier benefits (although clearly there may be a greater future impact if asset prices remain depressed in the medium term). Looking forward, from a political economy perspective, the fall in the value of funded pillar pensions because of the crisis may also have implications for the appetite for future reforms or calls for changes in the current structure of pension provision.

CHAPTER 2

Household Vulnerabilities

A. Introduction

This chapter examines household vulnerabilities by analyzing how macro shocks discussed in Chapter 1, namely (i) credit market shocks, (ii) external price (food and fuel) shocks, and (iii) income shocks, impact their well-being. It treats each of these shocks separately and quantifies how the crisis is likely affecting the welfare of households, on average, and, whenever possible and drawing from country-specific examples and illustrations, how such welfare effects may be distributed across households.

The results reported in this chapter suggest that household vulnerability in ECA is widespread. There are adverse effects on both poor households and nonpoor households depending on the macroeconomic shock, the specific transmission channel, and selected household characteristics. In brief, this chapter finds the following:

- *The ongoing macroeconomic shocks will significantly expand the pool of households that are unable to service their debt.*

Interest rate shocks in Estonia, Lithuania, and Hungary, for example, can increase the share of vulnerable households or borrowers at risk (in percentage of all indebted households) by up to 20 percentage points, depending on the magnitude and severity of the shock. Household indebtedness has risen rapidly in ECA countries among both poor and nonpoor households. The nature of household debt in ECA is such that many households have likely exposed themselves to various types of risks, including exchange rate and interest rate risks, with few opportunities for hedging.

- *The food and fuel crisis may not be over and a new round of price increases will have substantial effects on household welfare.* International commodity price levels have not returned to pre-2007 levels and falling currencies in some ECA countries are resulting in a new round of price increases, depending on the share of imported food and fuel in local consumption and the degree of pass-through of exchange rate changes in domestic prices. The net effect of a food price shock depends on whether households are net producers or net consumers of food, it depends on their intensity of food consumption and the availability of cheaper substitutes, and it depends on their livelihood strategies, access to agriculture assets and inputs, and ability to take advantage of profitable opportunities in agriculture. These multiple considerations suggest that, at least in principle, the poor are not necessarily the hardest hit. However, the food share of total household consumption typically falls with income and, in reality, the poor are also likely to be the worst hit, as many of the poor in Albania, Kyrgyz Republic, and Tajikistan, for example, are also observed to be net consumers, with limited access to agriculture assets and inputs.

- *Poverty will rise.* The region now risks a major reversal of its gains in the years of economic recovery following the 1998 Russian crisis. By 2010, about 11 million more people could fall into poverty and an additional 24 million people could find themselves vulnerable, or just above ECA's international poverty line, over the next two years. The regional simulations mask the heterogeneity of impact within countries, including the likely concentration of the poverty impact in selected economic sectors. Country studies recently completed suggest that for economic shocks transmitted primarily through the labor market, poverty will rise especially among households that have been dependent on remittance inflows and those previously employed in booming construction sectors where economic activity is now projected to decline sharply.

The rest of the chapter is organized as follows: Section B sets out the context for the analysis in terms of the trends in poverty reduction and vulnerability prior to the crisis.

Section C discusses the empirical strategy, the scope and objectives, and the key limitations of the analysis. Section D presents the results of the analysis of household indebtedness and the likely impact of credit market shocks on the household debt service burden in selected countries. Section E analyzes recent trends in food and fuel prices, patterns of food and fuel consumption among households in the region, and the likely impact on households of a new round of food and fuel prices increases. Section F assesses the impact of the regional recession and, in particular, the effect on household welfare of falling incomes in the region.

B.   Context: Poverty and Vulnerability in the Pre-Crisis Period

Over the recovery period following the 1998 Russian crisis through 2006, some 50 million people moved out of poverty in the region.[14] Poverty fell throughout all the sub-regions of ECA led by the middle-income countries of the CIS, which experienced the largest declines in poverty, particularly in Russia where the share of the poor and vulnerable has declined sharply in percentage of the population.

Poverty reduction in ECA has been driven largely by growth in average income. In particular, growth in mean income is calculated to have contributed close to 90 percent of the overall reduction in poverty experienced by the region. A modest improvement in the distribution of income has also helped reduce poverty. The labor market has provided an important channel for poverty reduction in the region, largely through rising real wages among the working poor. In contrast, job creation has generally not been an important factor for reducing poverty. For a number of countries, the index of employment has been flat in recent years.

Notwithstanding the rapid decreases in poverty, millions of people still remain poor or are just above the poverty line. More than two-thirds of the poor live in the middle-income countries of the region, including Kazakhstan, Poland, Romania, Russia, and Turkey. Not surprisingly, low-income countries in ECA have higher rates of poverty and vulnerability compared to other countries in the region, but as a group, they account for less than a quarter of the region's poor population.

The growth slowdown will have significant adverse consequences for the region, given its poverty and vulnerability profile. Most of the poor in the ECA region are working adults and children. Together, they represent about two-thirds of the poor population across countries in the region, with the working poor accounting for anywhere from about a quarter (e.g., Turkey) to close to half (middle-income CIS) of the poor population. The working poor represent a group that is directly exposed to the fall in income and declining employment prospects projected throughout the region. In addition, because many of those currently employed have just moved out of poverty, they are just above the poverty line and highly susceptible to modest falls in mean income and economic activity.

C. Shocks to Household Welfare: Empirical Strategy

The rest of this chapter examines household vulnerabilities using micro data by examining the potential impact of credit market shocks, external price (food and fuel) shocks, and income shocks on household welfare. The impact on household welfare is defined as the change in the household debt service burden, the fall in real income, or movements into poverty, as appropriate. The report presents regional overviews and simulations along with cross-country comparisons and contrasts. It also presents selected country examples, depending on data availability and relevant economic developments, to illustrate the incidence and distribution of specific vulnerabilities within countries.

The novel microeconomic analysis in the report draws on a large, cross-country database of household surveys. We use the most recent pre-crisis household data along with aggregate macroeconomic outturns to simulate the impact on households of key economic shocks already taking place. The report brings together for the first time comparable cross-country data on household indebtedness for a large group of ECA countries using the EU Survey of Income and Living Conditions (EU-SILC) and Household Budget Surveys (HBS). The report also highlights newly updated information on household consumption from the ECA Household Data Archives. Comparisons with Western Europe and other advanced economies are also used to inform the analysis when relevant data are available.

Important Caveats

The analysis is not exhaustive. First, the choice of emphasis has been guided in large part by the policy issues of the day when the project was first designed. Thus, for example, it is an analysis of food and fuel price shocks, instead of rising prices of other household consumption items, reflecting the widespread concern over the food and fuel crisis. It is an analysis of household indebtedness and the welfare consequences of rising debt burdens—rather than, for example, the analysis of the welfare effects of the continuing lack of access to credit among certain households—given the policy interest in the new vulnerabilities created by the credit boom through 2007–2008 in many countries in ECA. Second, the country examples and analyses have also been selective, depending on data availability and the relative country exposure and risk. This is a primary reason why the potential impact on household welfare of wealth changes associated with the crisis, such as those related to property and equity price falls, is not analyzed.

The analysis is not predictive. The GDP growth projections alone, on which many of the simulations here are predicated, were updated at least *three* times during the course of the preparation of this report. The frequency of updates reflects the substantial uncertainty regarding the severity and duration of the crisis and, by extension, its impact on households. In addition, the actual poverty impact can be mitigated by private responses to the crisis and by various household coping strategies. This study is unable to account for the interactions between channels, the behavioral changes (including coping strategies to mitigate the crisis, discussed in the final chapter), and the net higher-order effects. Policy responses, meanwhile, can either mitigate or exacerbate some of these consequences.

The results are not additive. The analyses of changes in household welfare in response to three types of shocks are treated as parallel exercises. First, the shocks have not been analyzed within a common general equilibrium framework. Second, the choice of country examples and illustrations vary across shocks, depending on data availability and the relevant country risk. More generally, the data are drawn from two different household data sources. Finally, there are methodological differences in the way vulnerability was evaluated, consistent with the respective existing literature. With household indebtedness, for example, the impact of the shocks is assessed relative to indicative debt burden "thresholds" (payments in percentage of income). With respect to the fall in income, the predicted household consumption levels are compared to an international poverty line. However, the real impacts in each country may very well be multi-channeled and cumulative. Countries in Eastern Europe, for example, have to deal with financial sector shocks and labor market shocks, as well as product market shocks transmitted through currency declines. For a number of reasons, however, we treat these impacts independently using partial equilibrium analysis.

The aim, then, is to provide a broad overview of household vulnerabilities confronted by the region. This report seeks to assess how such vulnerabilities are distributed across countries and, within countries, across broad types of households. Some of the estimated effects may be understated, as they capture only some of the first-round effects. On the other hand, general equilibrium effects will either dampen or worsen some of these effects.

This report is also cognizant of many ongoing, decentralized efforts throughout the region to simulate the household welfare consequences of the crisis. Such efforts are able to model these effects and interactions more fully using richer, more comprehensive country-specific data. This report does not substitute for those efforts—some of whose preliminary results are also reported and referenced below—but instead provides a complementary regional overview.

D. Households and Credit Market Shocks

Background

Household debt now represents a little over a quarter of GDP in the EU10. Though nontrivial, this level is lower than the debt level in most of the older EU member countries, which on average is about 65 percent of GDP. Within the EU10, however, there is significant variation in aggregate household debt holdings, in both their level and composition. Estonia is at the higher end of the distribution by magnitude, with household debt representing close to half of GDP. Household debt in percent of GDP in the CIS and other ECA countries, in turn, lags behind the EU10, on average. Ukraine is an exception, with household indebtedness comparable to that of the EU10 average.

As household financial positions have grown, there has been a shift toward housing loans or mortgages on the liability side of the balance sheet and an increasing share of equities and pension and mutual funds

FIGURE 2.1
Household Debt: Selected ECA Countries, 2008
In percent of GDP, end-period

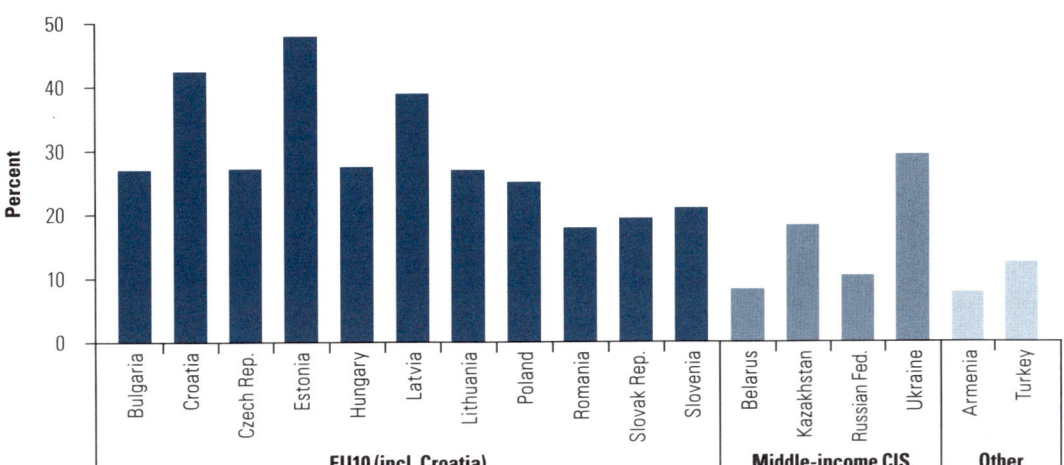

Sources: European Central Bank, National Central Banks, IMF, and UniCredit.

FIGURE 2.2
Growth in Mortgage Debt: Selected ECA Countries, 2007

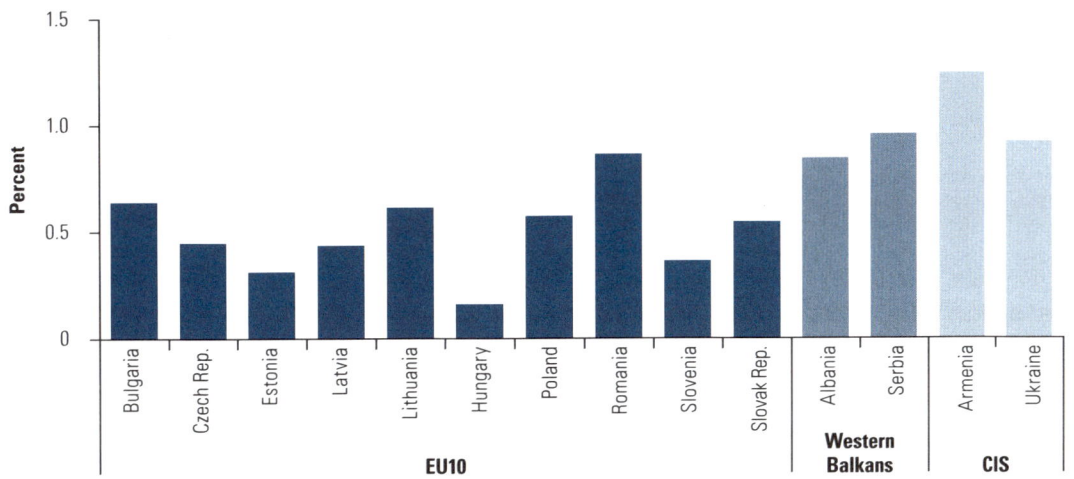

Source: European Mortgage Federation.

on the asset side. For many of the countries in ECA, rising mortgage and housing loans have accounted for much of the growth in household liabilities and now, for example, account for around 40 percent of total household liabilities in Bulgaria, Croatia, and Hungary and up to 60 percent in the Czech Republic. However, for some notable exceptions, such as Romania and Bulgaria, consumer credit remains the primary form of household loans. Elsewhere, such as in the CIS, housing loans are a much smaller share of all household loans compared to the EU10. Mortgage debt has increased multiple times over the period 2002–2007 both in per capita terms and relative to disposable income. Some have suggested that government initiatives, such as construction or mortgage-related subsidy and tax schemes, have contributed to this growth.

The growth in mortgages can also be viewed in terms of longer-term convergence toward the financial norms of Western Europe. Indeed, as would be expected, the most rapid annualized growth over the period 2002 to 2007 was seen in those economies with relative low initial levels of mortgages per capita. At 2007, housing loans accounted for close to 60 percent of all household loans. Mortgage debt in Serbia, for example, grew at an astonishing rate of 96 percent in 2007 while growing by 86 percent in Albania. In Russia, the Central Bank reports that mortgage lending grew by a factor of 2.6 in 2007.[15] CIS mortgage lending also grew very sharply.

FIGURE 2.3
The Composition of Household Debt
In percent of total

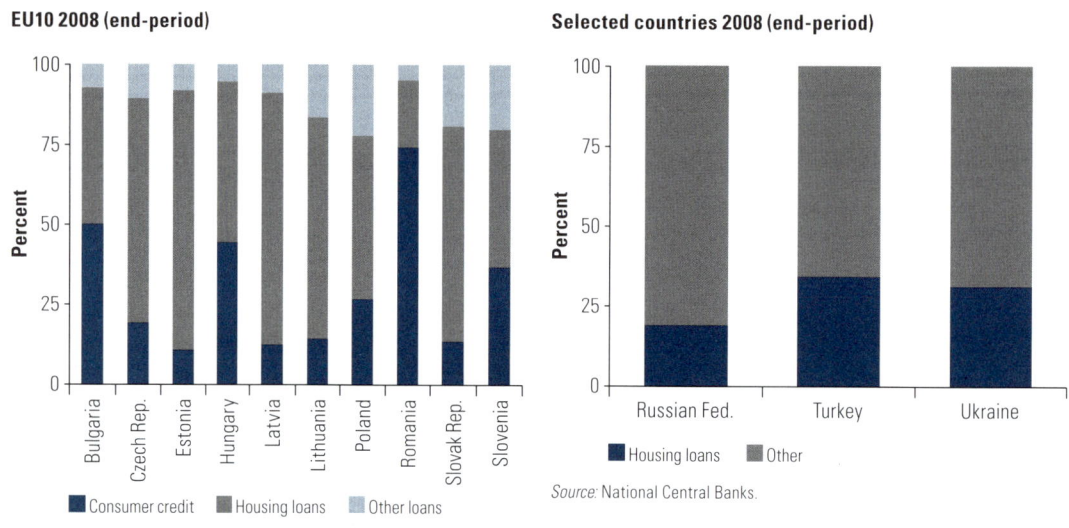

Source: European Central Bank.

Source: National Central Banks.

FIGURE 2.4
Latvia Household Loan Delinquency Rates and Unemployment Rate

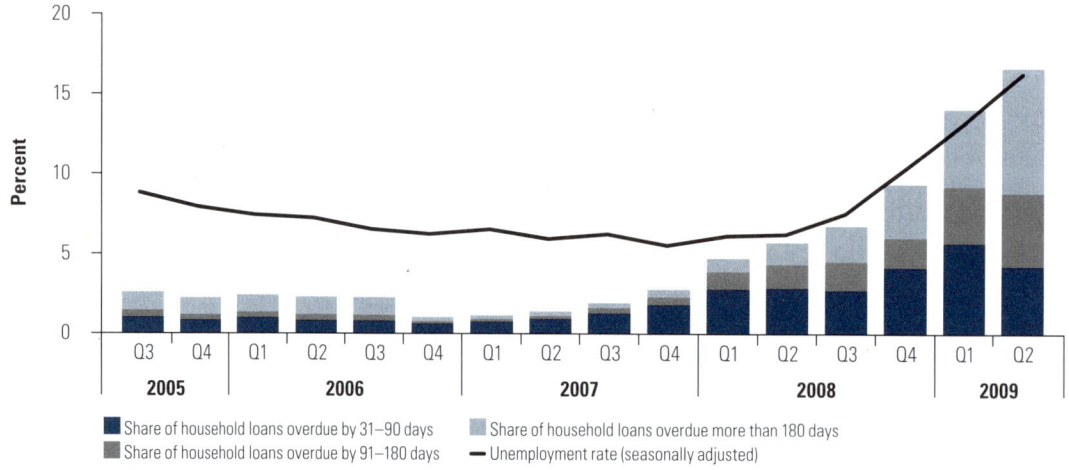

Sources: Eurostat and the Financial and Capital Market Commission, Latvia.

The welfare consequences of rising house-hold indebtedness in the ECA region can be significant. Rising indebtedness reflects the benefits of financial sector development, allow-ing households to smooth their consumption over time and acquire home ownership without significant savings. In fact, there exists a grow-ing literature on the welfare impact of credit *constraints* among households, particularly in a downturn when households are unable to meet their consumption needs.[16] On the other hand, rapidly growing household indebtedness and the exposure of the financial sector to vulner-able households (or borrowers at risk) may have important consequences for financial stability. At the same time, the welfare and distribu-tional implications for households themselves can be large, particularly in a worsening mac-roeconomic environment.

Some characteristics of household debt in ECA expose these households to a number of macroeconomic shocks. Given these charac-teristics, household debt service burdens may increase in a difficult macroeconomic envi-ronment, and this in turn may lead to higher default and delinquency rates. These in turn

adversely affect the health of financial sector balance sheets with second-round implications for households in terms of the availability and cost of credit. Already, rising household loan delinquency ratios are being observed in some countries, as unemployment rates have risen.

First, a large share of household debt is denominated in foreign currencies or is indexed to foreign currencies, which has exposed house-holds to recent exchange rate depreciations to the extent that the currency composition of their assets, particularly their labor income flows, leaves them unhedged. Where foreign currency loans became popular in recent years, borrowers were typically obtaining loans in Euros and Swiss francs, attracted to relatively lower nominal interest rates compared to loans denominated in local currency.[17] On the banks' side, at the height of the expansion in household credit, there appeared little interest in reducing their exposure to foreign-currency-denomi-nated loans because default rates were low and because of the ease of access, at the time, to for-eign currency funding via wholesale markets or via Western European parent banks. Among households borrowing in foreign currency,

FIGURE 2.5

Foreign-Currency-Denominated Loans, 2008

In percent of bank loans to households

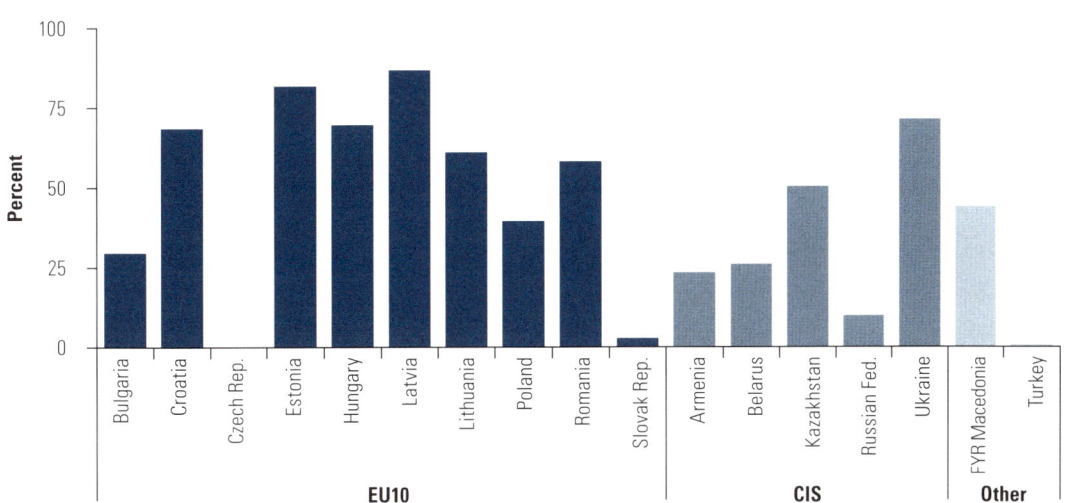

Sources: MNB and other National Central Banks.

FIGURE 2.6
Foreign-Currency-Denominated Loans in Ukraine, 2008
In percent of total, by currency

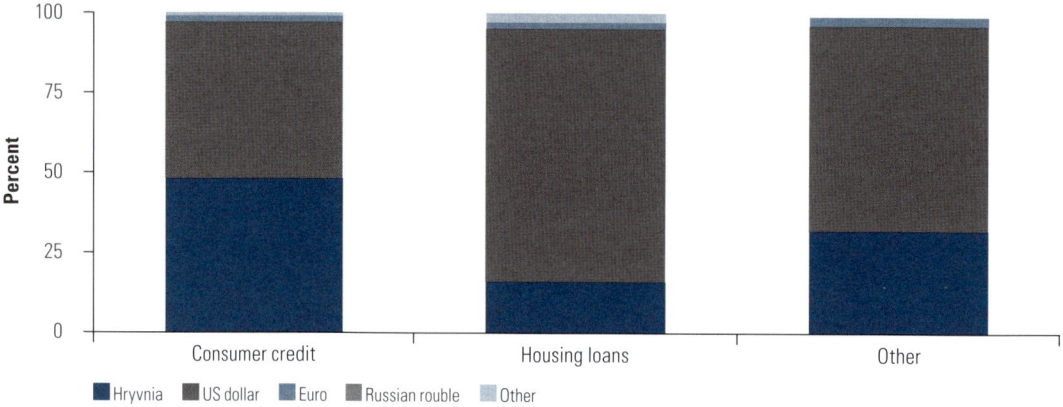

Sources: National Bank of Ukraine and staff calculations.

however, there also seemed little awareness of their exposure to currency risks although in some countries a high share of foreign currency deposits provides some hedging of the currency risk. These developments in the EU10 mirror recent trends elsewhere, particularly in the middle-income CIS countries, where households also obtained loans denominated in US dollars and other foreign currencies. In Serbia, few of the household loans are explicitly foreign-currency-denominated. However, up to 81 percent appear to be foreign-currency-indexed.[18]

There are again substantial variations in the foreign currency exposures of household debt across countries. The Baltics and Ukraine are at the higher end of this distribution, with foreign-currency-denominated loans accounting for over 80 percent of bank loans to households in Estonia and Latvia; the Czech and Slovak Republics are at the lower end, with little or no foreign-currency-denominated household debt. Some have suggested that a few national policies may explain some of these differences across countries—such as more restricted eligibility requirements in 2004 for housing subsidies in Hungary (which then prompted households to substitute toward less expensive foreign currency loans) or regulatory measures to limit borrowing foreign currency in the Czech Republic.[19]

Second, in some EU10 countries, mortgages with variable (adjustable) interest rates account for the largest share of lending, exposing households to interest rate shocks. In these countries, such variable interest rate mortgage debt represented over three-quarters of all mortgage debt, at least until recently, using available data. Households are vulnerable in a financial downturn, in the event that banks pass on a higher cost of credit to them. However, as shown in other countries' experiences, this may be mitigated to the extent that interest rate adjustments may be capped, as is the case, for example, in Denmark.

Increasing mortgage indebtedness has exposed a rising share of households to the recent changes in house price trends in many of the EU10 countries. For example, in Estonia and Latvia house prices fell in Q4 2008 by around 16 percent and 36 percent year-on-year respectively compared with growth rates of around 20 percent and 60 percent in Q1 2007. Such price changes lead to redistributions of wealth between those long or short in housing stocks. These can then affect the distribution of consumption via direct wealth effects and via the impacts of changing collateral values on credit constraints. Indeed, household-level analysis in the United Kingdom has found the

FIGURE 2.7
Mortgage Loans with Adjustable Interest Rates, 2006
In percent of all housing loans

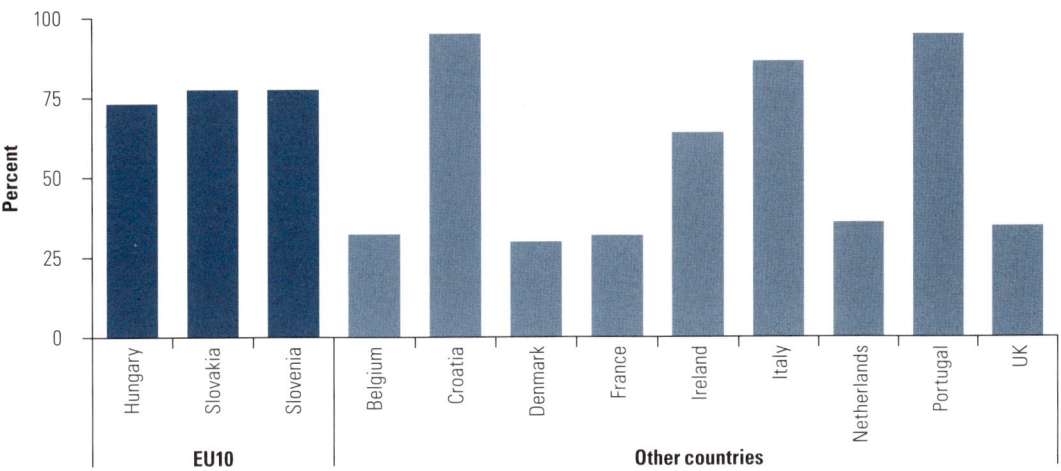

Sources: IMF, OECD, and National Central Banks.

largest elasticity of consumption with respect to housing prices in older homeowners with an insignificant elasticity for younger renters.[20]

Household Vulnerability:
Regional Overview

Microeconomic data can be a critical source of information on household indebtedness. Current assessments of the credit risks faced by the banking sector have been largely based on macroeconomic data. In general, little is known about household indebtedness based on household-level data in the EU10. The debt profile could vary across household income groups and by type of loan, such as mortgage and non-mortgage. In principle, such micro-economic data and profiles allow for a closer monitoring of risks associated with selected household groups. Where household borrowing is limited, indicators based on average household indebtedness for all households as a whole mask the likely concentration of borrowing among selected households.

This section draws information from the databases of the EU-SILC, an annual household survey anchored in the European Statistical System that was first initiated in 2003, with the new EU member countries undertaking their first surveys in 2005. Data are typically made available to the general public two years after the survey, so we currently have data through 2007 and data for both older and newer EU members for 2005–2007. Among other variables, the EU-SILC collects information on the incidence of mortgage debt holding, interest payments, arrears on mortgage interest payments, and disposable income. The analysis of EU-SILC data is supplemented with the analysis of a few other ECA countries with relevant variables in their HBS. For these countries, there is information on total household debt, including mortgage debt and other household loans, and on total debt service, including interest payment and principal payment, in contrast to the EU-SILC data, which has information on interest payment alone.

There are a few notable patterns in the household survey data, suggesting likely adverse welfare consequences during an economic downturn. These include patterns of household debt holdings, including among those that are more vulnerable or less able to service their debt in a difficult economic environment.

BOX 1

Definition of EU-SILC Variables Used in the Analysis

Total disposable household income is the sum for all household members of gross personal income components (gross employee cash or near cash income; gross non-cash employee income; gross cash benefits or losses from self-employment [including royalties]; unemployment benefits; old-age benefits; survivor's benefits; sickness benefits; disability benefits; and education-related allowances) *plus* gross income components at household level (income from rental of a property or land; family/children-related allowances; social exclusion not elsewhere classified; housing allowances; regular inter-household cash transfers received; interests, dividends, profit from capital investments in unincorporated business; income received by people aged under 16) *minus* regular taxes on wealth; regular inter-household cash transfer paid; and tax on income and social insurance contributions.

Interest paid on mortgage refers to the total gross amount, before deducting any tax credit or tax allowance, of mortgage interest on the main residence of the household during the income reference period. It excludes any other mortgage payments, either interest or principal, made at the same time, such as mortgage protection insurance or home and contents insurance; payments on mortgages to obtain money for housing purposes (e.g., repairs, renovations, maintenance) or for non-housing purposes; and repayments of the principal or capital sum.

Reproduced from Eurostat, *Description of SILC User Database Variables.* Version 2007.1 (01-03-09). Permission being requested.

First, debt holdings rise with household income level but are spread across income quintiles, including the poorer households. In the Czech Republic, for example, over a third of households in the poorest quintile hold some debt, rising to about 55 percent of households in the richest quintile. In addition, on average among EU10 countries, the share of mortgage holders across age groups first increases and then decreases with age, a pattern that is broadly consistent with the life cycle theory of consumer behavior. Taken together, these suggest that when macroeconomic shocks increase the financial burden due to mortgage debt, it is the poorest households and the youngest households with weaker ties to the labor market who are among those most likely to suffer adverse shocks, in the absence of a savings buffer. The shocks can be channeled through income shocks, exchange rate shocks (if the mortgage is in foreign currency), or interest rate shocks (in case of variable-interest mortgages). If the mortgage payments represent a considerable share of a household's disposable income, a rising debt burden may curtail the household's ability to protect its welfare.

Second, in some countries debt service is a significant share of income, particularly among the poor. In Hungary, for example, data from the EU-SILC suggest that mortgage interest payments among the poor represent over 10 percent of their income. In Latvia, the share increases to almost 15 percent. If anything, these estimates of the debt service burden may be understated. A recent, independent survey for UniCredit Group indicates that for about 30 percent of all households, total household debt repayment covers more than a fifth of the household budget. Another 20 percent of households allocate 10 to 20 percent of their household budget to debt repayments.

Third, in some countries, mortgage interest payments are a significant share of income

FIGURE 2.8
Household Debt by Income Quintile
In percent of households

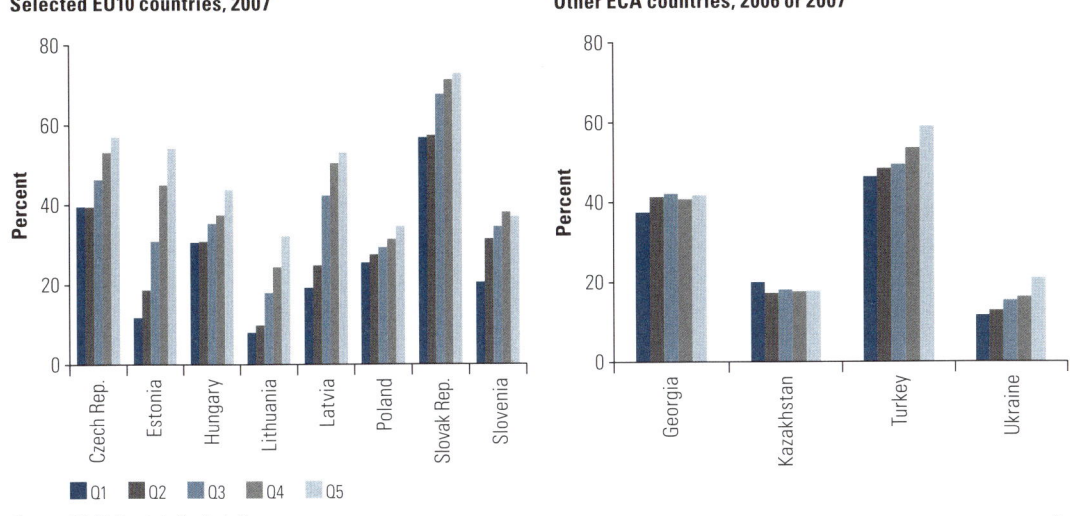

Sources: EU-SILC and staff calculations.

FIGURE 2.9
Household Income Used for Debt Repayments
In percent of all households

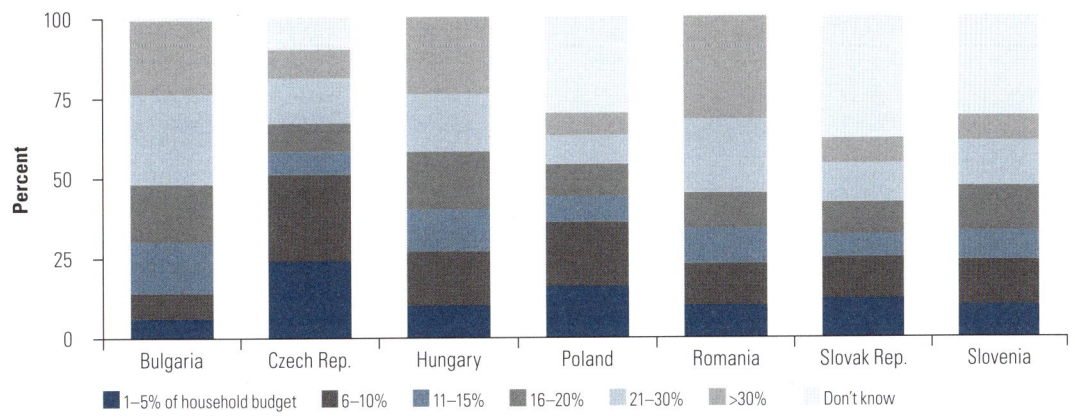

Source: UniCredit Group.

Note: The graph should be read as follows: The bars represent shares of the household population. The colors represent the percentage of household budget spent on debt service. In Slovenia, for example, 10 percent of households spend 1 to 5 percent of their budgets on debt service. Another 15 percent of households allocate 6 to 10 percent of their budgets for debt service.

among the youngest and oldest workers. In Hungary, the youngest workers (age 25 and younger) allocate over a tenth of their disposable household income to mortgage interest payments. Slovak workers in the youngest group also spend almost 10 percent of their income to pay mortgage interest. In Lithuania, interest payments as a share of disposable income are the smallest in the youngest workers and then rise with age, reaching close to 6 percent of income among those aged 55 or older. In the meanwhile, in Latvia, mortgage interest payments occupy a large share of household income across all age groups from the youngest to oldest, which is, in most cases, over 10 percent of disposable income. Large debt service ratios are also observed among those employed in economic sectors that have experienced some of the sharpest downturns in recent months (such as in construction).

Stress Testing Household Indebtedness: Country Illustrations

Introduction

Stress tests of household debt using microeconomic data are rare, but the results of existing tests suggest considerable welfare consequences. A recent stress test in Hungary suggests that a simultaneous fall in employment and an interest rate shock would increase "risky loans" by 8 to 12 percentage points. Though the banking sector is found to be resilient to these shocks, the default risk is concentrated among the poor households. A stress test in Poland suggests that unemployment shocks (compared to interest rate or exchange rate shocks) have the highest impact on probability of default. Modest increases in unemployment can increase the share of loans in default by over 5 percentage points.[21]

We ran similar analyses of mortgage debt on a few selected countries, using EU-SILC data, and of total household debt, using HBS data. The choice of countries has been guided by data availability and the degree of exposure to interest rate, exchange rate, and unemployment rate shocks. The magnitude of the hypothetical shocks has been driven by actual changes in recent months—such as the doubling of unemployment rates in some EU10 countries—and is thus greater in magnitude than what has been previously assumed by the few stress tests that exist. We also simulated uniform shocks across countries—for example, 25 percent exchange rate depreciations—as explained more fully in Box 2.

For two of the countries analyzed, the fixed exchange rate regime, the authorities' commitment to the peg, and the credibility of this regime protect households from the adverse effects of exchange rate adjustments. Some institutions have been examining the merits of alternative exchange rate regimes and they argue that a regime change would lead to adverse social consequences.[22] *The results of the simulations here should be seen in a similar light, as evidence of the likely welfare costs of abandoning the peg.*

BOX 2

Stress Testing Household Indebtedness

This section follows some recent attempts to stress test household debt holding and assess the share (or change in share) of vulnerable households.[23] The steps taken are outlined as follows:

Calculating baseline figures. First, we use data from a sample of households from selected household surveys to calculate some baseline figures for the debt service burden (which may or may not include principal repayments, depending on the data source).

Identifying vulnerable households. Second, the debt service burden is compared to an indicative threshold, against which a household may be classified as vulnerable. There are two principal ways of defining indicative thresholds for determining the increase in the number of vulnerable households (sometimes referred to as "borrowers at risk"):

BOX 2 *(continued)*

Stress Testing Household Indebtedness

(i)   One is based on the notion of a **"financial margin,"** or the disposable income left after deducting debt payments and basic living costs.[24] Households with negative margins are considered to be in financial distress and are likely to default on their debts. We use this benchmark in analyzing the HBS data on the total debt service burden.

(ii) The other measure is an indicative **threshold debt service** burden that is more arbitrary, and based on previous findings regarding the level at which a household is more likely to become delinquent or be in arrears. In particular, we compare EU-SILC data on interest payments as a share of disposable income to an indicative threshold of 20 percent, following previous studies of mortgage delinquencies.[25] We also use a 30 percent threshold in our sensitivity tests.

Subjecting households to shocks. Third, the households are subjected to various macroeconomic shocks, such as an interest rate shock, an exchange rate shock, and an unemployment shock. The magnitude of the shock—such as some percentage point increase in the aggregate unemployment rate—depends on a country's own historical increase, over the most recent two-year period.[26] In addition, we use two hypothetical scenarios, as listed below. The selection of specific households subjected to a shock proceeds as follows:

In the case of an **unemployment shock,** the selection of a particular household that is subjected to the shock—that is, whether a given household member becomes jobless—can be either random or based on a probability model of unemployment. In the case of a random assignment, we employ 1,000 draws and then calculate the average outcome, including the standard error.[27] In the case of a probability assignment, the likelihood of being unemployed is drawn from a probit model of unemployment, where unemployment is a function of an individual's socioeconomic background, demographic characteristics, and geographic location. We employ a parsimonious model and assume that there are four key drivers of the probability of unemployment: educational level, age, gender, and place of residence.[28]

In the case of an **interest rate shock,** we use aggregate figures on the share of variable interest loans out of all household loans (e.g., 40 percent of all loans have adjustable interest rates). We adopt one critical assumption: we assume that loans with variable interest rates are proportionally distributed across indebted households, such that where, for example, 40 percent of all loans are variable interest rate loans, then we assume that 40 percent of all indebted households have variable interest rate loans. This is admittedly a crude assumption, as household debt with variable interest rates may be concentrated among selected groups of households. However, in the absence of more detailed information in household surveys on interest rate variability of each household's debt holding, this is the most reasonable assumption we could make.[29] The share of households with variable interest loans is randomly selected using a similar routine outlined above, and these households are then subjected to the relevant interest rate shock. As before, we employ 1,000 draws and calculate the average outcome.

In the case of an **exchange rate shock,** the selection of households follows the same general procedure outlined above in the preceding paragraph.

BOX 2 *(continued)*

Stress Testing Household Indebtedness

The magnitude of the hypothesized shock. As previously stated we simulate the impact of shocks based on actual changes in recent years as well as on uniform, hypothesized magnitudes. In the case of unemployment rates, for example, some Baltic countries have experienced as much as 10 percentage point increases in the unemployment rate. We use these actual changes as base cases as well as a uniform 10 and 15 percentage point increase across countries. In the case of interest rate shocks, countries in our sample have experienced 2 to 4 percentage point maximum increases in recent years. In addition, we also simulate 3, 5, and 6 percentage point increases. A 3 percentage point stress test is typical in the household debt literature, but other have simulated more severe shocks such as 5 and 6 percentage point increases as well.[30] Finally, in the case of exchange rate shocks, we use maximum actual changes (which have been substantial in a few cases) as well as a uniform 25 and 35 percent depreciation. For selected countries with SILC data, we are able to simulate interest rate, exchange rate, and unemployment shocks. For countries with HBS, we do not have the necessary information on the share of loans with variable interest rates.

Recalculating the share of vulnerable households. As households are subjected to a shock—for example, as a member of the household becomes "unemployed" and ceases to receive any income from work[31]—the shock then results in the decrease in total household income and the household's ability to repay debt. In the case of an interest rate shock or an exchange rate shock, the size of debt (or interest) payment grows accordingly. In all cases, the debt service burden is recalculated and then compared to the relevant threshold. The share of vulnerable households then rises accordingly.

Results

The results of the analysis of EU-SILC data suggest that current macroeconomic shocks can significantly expand the pool of households that are unable to service their debt. A severe 5 percentage point interest rate shock in Estonia, Lithuania, and Hungary, for example, can increase the share of vulnerable households or borrowers at risk by up to 20 percentage points, depending on the magnitude and severity of the shock (figure 2.10). A less restrictive threshold—that is, interest payment representing 30 percent of disposable income—yields smaller welfare effects from interest rate shocks compared to this first set of estimates, but they are still large. In particular, the share of borrowers at risk can expand by 7 to 12 percentage points in our sample of countries. A more modest interest rate hike—3 percentage points—using a 30 percent threshold yields much lower but still nontrivial adverse consequences for household well-being. Borrowers at risk increase by 4 to 7 percentage points of all indebted households. The results are in appendix table 1, appendix table 2, and appendix table 3.

Unemployment shocks also expand the share of vulnerable households by several percentage points. The results hold, regardless of whether the unemployment shock follows a probability assignment or a random assignment, although a random assignment generally leads to higher welfare costs.

In the countries analyzed, interest rate shocks have the largest impact on household vulnerability. In part, this is due to the assumed magnitude of the shock. It is also driven by the

FIGURE 2.10

Stress Testing Household Indebtedness: Selected EU-SILC Data

Vulnerable households or borrowers at risk as a share of indebted households

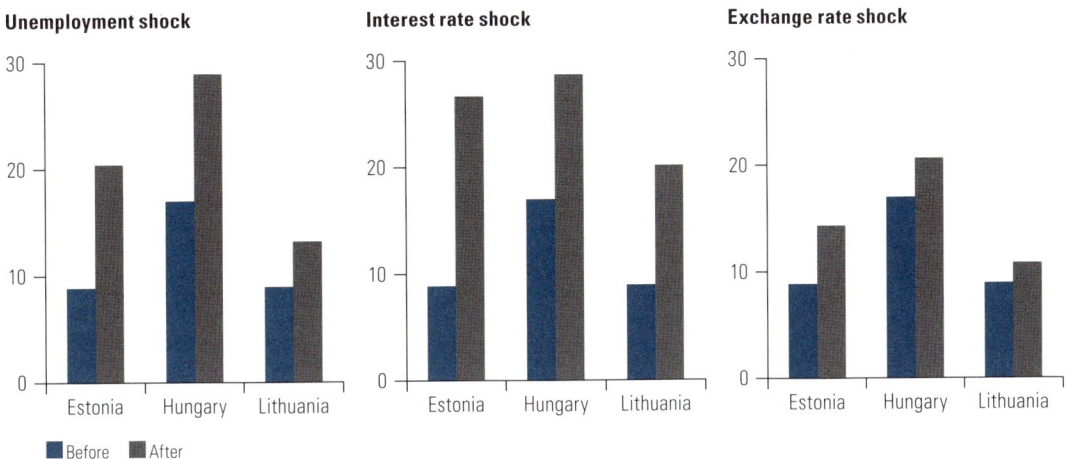

Sources: EU-SILC data and staff calculations.

Note: The simulated shocks are a 10 percentage point increase in unemployment rates, a 5 percentage point increase in interest rate shocks, and 25 percent depreciation in exchange rates. This refers to mortgage debt only. Vulnerable households are identified using a 20 percent interest payment threshold. See main text and Box 2.

degree of initial exposure. In particular, while only *some* indebted households will be hit by an unemployment shock, *all* indebted households with variable interest rates will see increasing debt burdens from an interest rate hike.

The analysis of HBS data assuming comparable unemployment and exchange rate shocks suggests a far more limited impact on household welfare.[32] In Belarus, Kazakhstan, Serbia, and Ukraine, exchange rate shocks increase,

FIGURE 2.11

Stress Testing Household Indebtedness: Selected HBS Data

Vulnerable households or borrowers at risk as a share of indebted households

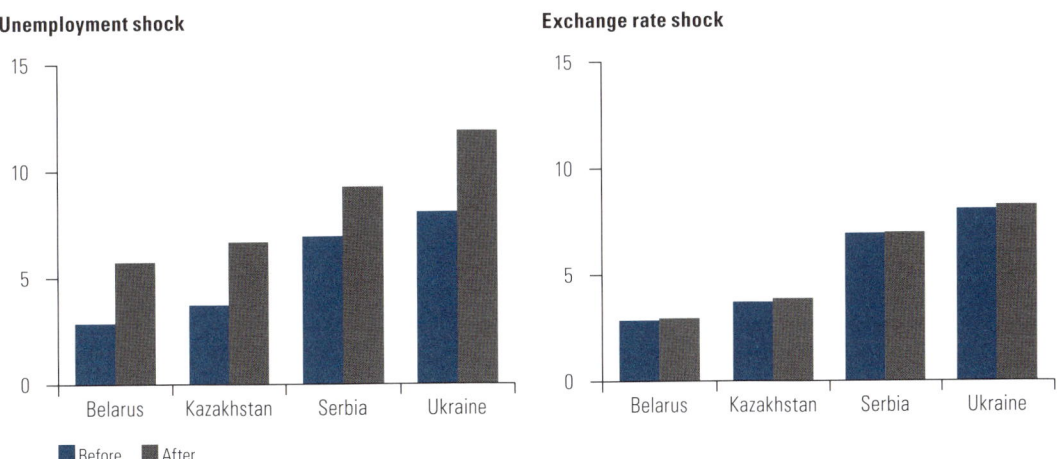

Sources: HBS data and staff calculations.

Note: The simulated shocks are a 10 percentage point increase in unemployment rates and a 25 percent depreciation in exchange rates. Vulnerable households are identified based on the "financial margin" measure. See main text and Box 2.

on average, the share of borrowers at risk by less than 1 percentage point. Unemployment rate shocks, on the other hand, were found to increase vulnerable households by up to 5 to 6 percentage points, depending on the magnitude of the shock and depending on whether the shocks are distributed randomly or according to a probability assignment.

These two sets of estimates—one for SILC and one for HBS—are not comparable. As previously discussed, one is based on mortgage debt information and the other is on total household debt. The two methodologies employed for identifying borrowers at risk—the use of a threshold level of interest payment burden in the case of SILC data

---

BOX 3

EU-SILC and HBS Data on Household Debt: Comparisons with Other Sources

This chapter uses household debt data drawn from EU-SILC and HBS data for those ECA countries for which the relevant data are available. Some caution is warranted in the interpretation of these household survey data, as they are not primarily designed to collect information on household liabilities. The focus of the SILC survey is not access to financial services or financing constraints, but rather social exclusion and income poverty. Because these are survey data, the volume of household loans and mortgages may not necessarily correspond fully to aggregate data from the banking sector. Nonetheless, in countries where SILC data have been analyzed, the data have provided a useful statistical portrait of the distribution of household debt.[33] More important, the calculations used in this chapter are broadly consistent with other sources of macroeconomic and microeconomic information.

First, *the trends in the share of households with negative financial margins are consistent with aggregate macroeconomic developments.* In Belarus, for example, between 2001 and 2008, the economy grew rapidly while poverty rates sharply. According to the National Bank's Bulletin of Banking Statistics, household and aggregate NPL ratios also declined. In our calculations of financial margins, the share of households with negative margins was also small and fell steadily between 2001 and 2008 (appendix figure 2). In Kazakhstan, more recent household survey data obtained by the team indicates that the share of household with negative margins began rising as the crisis hit the country in late 2007.

Second, *the socio-economic and demographic patterns of household debt holding documented here are consistent with other existing analyses of household debt data.* In Lithuania, for example, summary data from Bank of Lithuania indicate that the share of households with housing loans rises with income, consistent with EU-SILC patterns. More generally, the patterns of debt holding by income and by age in ECA countries for which data are available are fully consistent with those of Western Europe and other advanced economies.[34]

Third, for the Western European countries for which we have SILC data, *the relative ranking of countries in the share of indebted households is consistent with those of other sources,* such as the European Central Bank and OECD. Greece and Italy are at the lower end of the distribution while Netherlands is at the higher end.

BOX 3 *(continued)*

EU-SILC and HBS Data on Household Debt: Comparisons with Other Sources

The Share of Indebted Households: EU-SILC and ECB Data

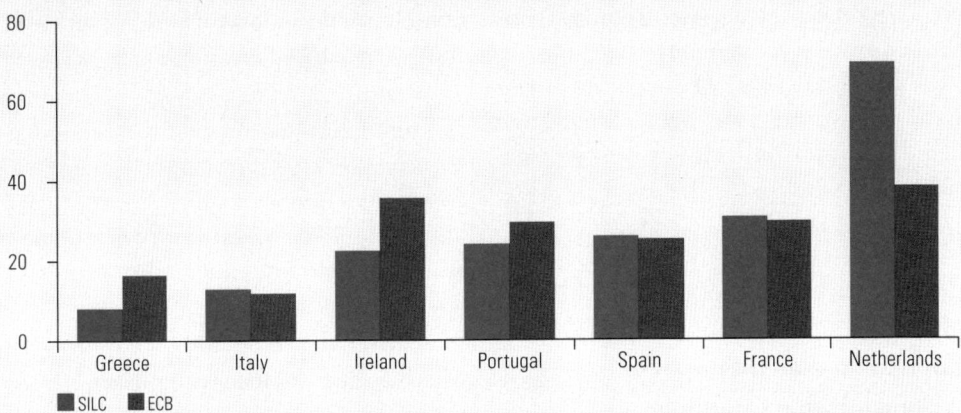

Nonetheless, in some countries *there are significant differences in the estimated levels of household indebtedness* as can be seen in the figure. There are also differences in the estimated debt service burden, where EU-SILC data for ECA countries can be compared with those of other studies.

For example, the debt service numbers calculated by the Bank of Slovakia, particularly for the poorest households, are several factors higher than those reported in this chapter; it is not clear what is driving the differences. Meanwhile, the debt service burden estimated by UniCredit (figure 2.9) is much higher relative to estimates from the EU-SILC for the same group of countries. In part, it could reflect the deteriorating household financial conditions captured by UniCredit's more recent data collection efforts. They may also be explained by differences in survey design, though information on UniCredit's survey design is not readily available. The results of the stress tests in this chapter could then be possibly a lower bound.

Debt Service: SILC and Unicredit Data

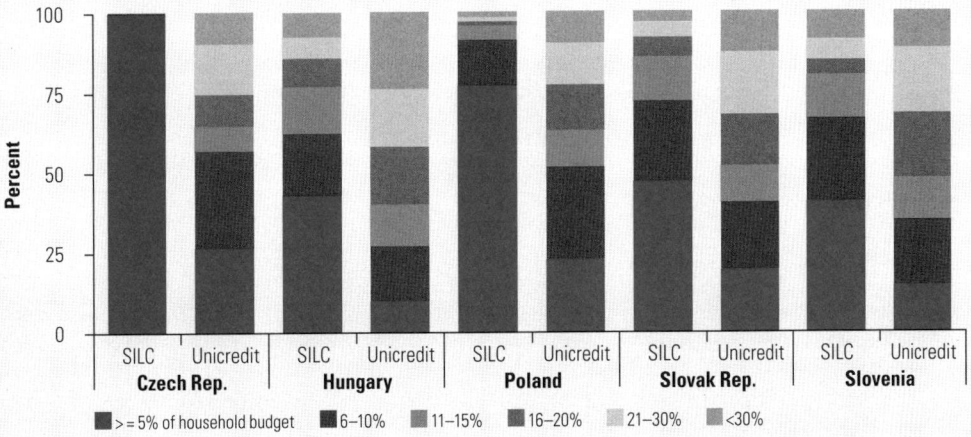

and the use of financial margins in the case of HBS data, which is a less restrictive measure of vulnerability—preclude a meaningful comparison of the two sets of outcomes. Nonetheless, some of the differences in the relative magnitudes may be driven in part by the differences in average debt burdens in these countries. In many of the countries with HBS data, the share of borrowers at risk is small, the average loan size is small, and the debt burdens are still sufficiently far from critical thresholds.

E. Households and External Price Shocks

Economic and Welfare Impact: Main Transmission Channels

The economic and welfare impact of rising commodity prices depends on the intensity of use. One possible index is "energy intensity," which is measured as energy consumption per unit of real GDP. Country averages over the past four decades indicate that energy intensity in advanced economies has fallen and both

emerging and developing countries are now substantially more energy-intensive in relative terms.[35] Similarly, food consumption is significantly higher in both emerging and developing countries compared to advanced economies. Their food consumption levels (in percent of household consumption) are almost three times those of advanced economies.

Where the price shock is transmitted through falling currencies, the economic consequence depends on whether a country is a net commodity importer. With respect to net food importing, some recent work based on an indicative threshold for vulnerability suggests that a few countries in ECA may be vulnerable.

Soaring domestic food and fuel prices—whether due to increasing global commodity food prices or falling currencies—affects the national headline inflation based on these commodities' share in a country's CPI. The relative importance of these commodities varies across countries, though some comparisons are hampered by the differences in the definition of what constitutes "food" (e.g., including or excluding beverage, tobacco, and others) and

FIGURE 2.12
Energy Intensity and Food Consumption, 1970s–2000s

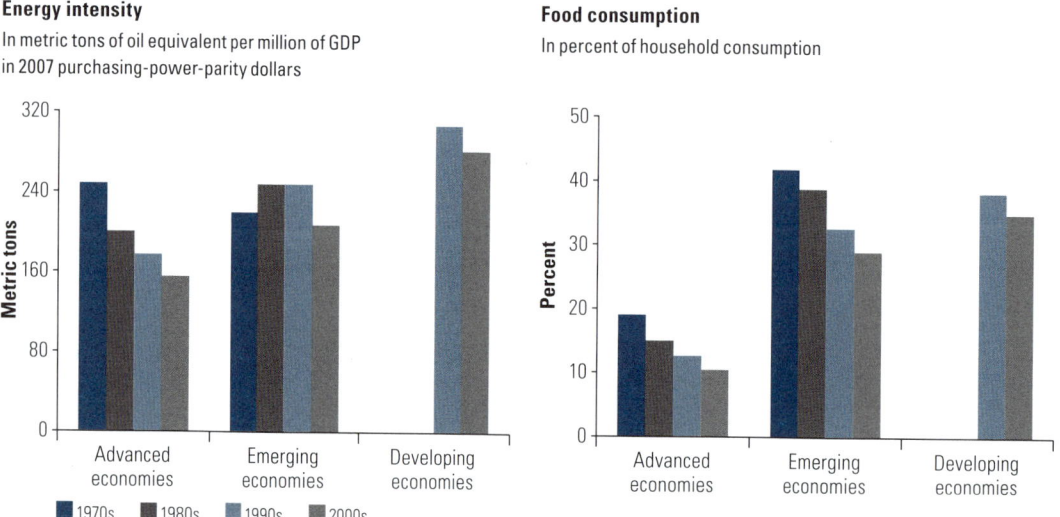

Energy intensity
In metric tons of oil equivalent per million of GDP in 2007 purchasing-power-parity dollars

Food consumption
In percent of household consumption

Legend: ■ 1970s ■ 1980s ■ 1990s ■ 2000s

Source: IMF 2008a.

"fuel" (e.g., including gasoline, household utilities, and others).

Notwithstanding these measurement issues, these commodities typically account for a large share of the consumption basket, particularly in poorer countries. Food represents about 10 percent of the consumption basket in richer countries, while representing up to 80 percent of the consumption basket in the world's poorest countries. Fuel accounts for a much smaller share, although this does not capture the secondary dimensions, that is, the use of fuel as input into the production of other items in the consumption basket. Evidence in some countries suggests that taken all together, both the primary and secondary use of fuel could

FIGURE 2.13
Food and Fuel Share of the CPI Basket

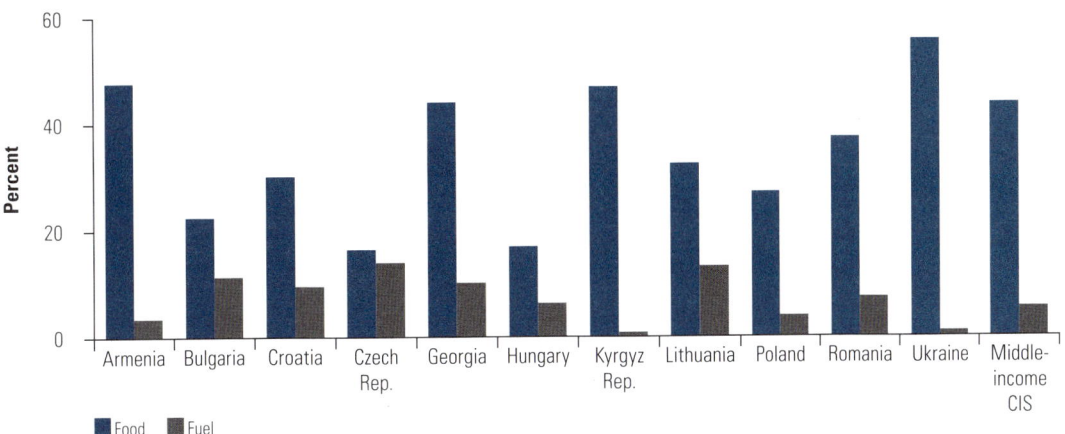

Sources: Kotaro Ishi and RES.

FIGURE 2.14
Food and Fuel Imports, 2006
In percent of GDP

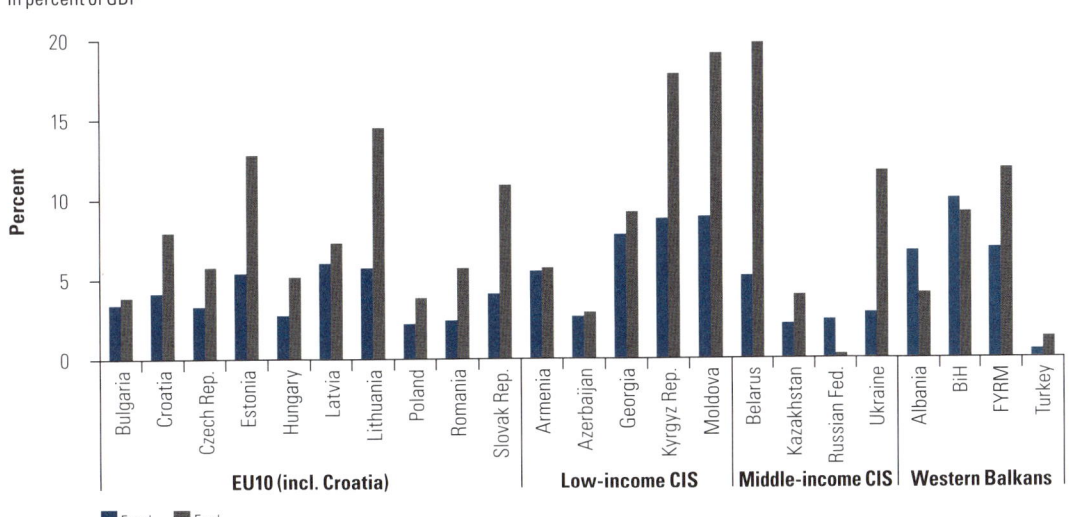

Sources: Habermeier et al. 2009 and IMF 2008b.

account for about double its typical share of the consumption basket.[36]

These aggregate economic effects hide some of the likely distributional consequences of commodity price shocks within countries. First, within a given country, the food share in the CPI consumption basket may understate the relative weight of food consumption among poorer households. Second, the poverty and social consequences may vary depending on the geographic location of the household and depending on whether households are net food buyers or net food sellers. It may also matter whether they rely exclusively on food purchases for food consumption and, if they do, whether they have access to cheaper substitutes. The rural poor are thought to be more self-sufficient, able to produce food for own-consumption, compared to the urban poor. With respect to energy consumption, the poor are also thought to have access to less expensive sources of energy (though they are probably dirtier sources and pose both environmental and health risks).

The indirect effects can also be large. Fuel price increases can have a direct poverty effect, through the household consumption of energy. The indirect effects on other products consumed by the households—using fuel as an intermediate input—can also be substantial. Studies of non-ECA countries suggest that fuel price increases can have net effects that are progressive (and thus have much larger welfare consequences for urban and richer households compared to poorer, rural households) mainly through their indirect effects.[37] The indirect effects through income can also be substantial. For households with members who are wage-employed in the agriculture sector, the increase in earnings may partially offset the welfare consequences of rising food prices.

Policy responses, in turn, may mute the effects of global commodity price shocks on domestic prices, though they may incur large fiscal costs or redistribute income regressively.

Governments may prevent a less-than-full pass through of higher prices to consumers, through lower fuel taxes or higher subsidies. Some countries use trade policy to address external price shocks. In 2008, for example, many countries enacted more restrictive food trade policy—such as through quantitative export restrictions and taxes on selected commodities—with the stated objective of protecting food security and curbing price increases. Though this may dampen overall price increases, the policy redistributes income away from net food sellers to net food buyers. Where net food sellers are mostly poorer, agricultural households, the policy impact can be regressive.

Regional Overview

The rise in food and fuel prices through 2008 has had adverse economic effects on countries in the region. For oil-importing countries, increases in energy prices led to widening trade imbalances and escalating inflationary pressures.[38] Higher energy prices also led to higher unit costs, which are perceived to undermine competitiveness unless accompanied by productivity enhancements. The poverty impact of further increases in food and fuel prices depends, as previously stated, on their relative importance in the consumption basket of households. Such shares of total consumption are observed to vary across countries and geographic locations and by household income, among other dimensions.

This section draws from the ECA Household Data Archives to assess household welfare consequences in case of a new round of price shocks. The figures below, for example, report the share of food and energy in total consumption by household quintiles in selected ECA countries (figure 2.15 and figure 2.16). There are a few notable observations:

First, as expected, richer countries have lower food shares. For example, food represents about a third of total consumption among the new EU member countries, on average. Among

FIGURE 2.15
Food Shares of Consumption
In percent of total consumption, by quintiles of household consumption

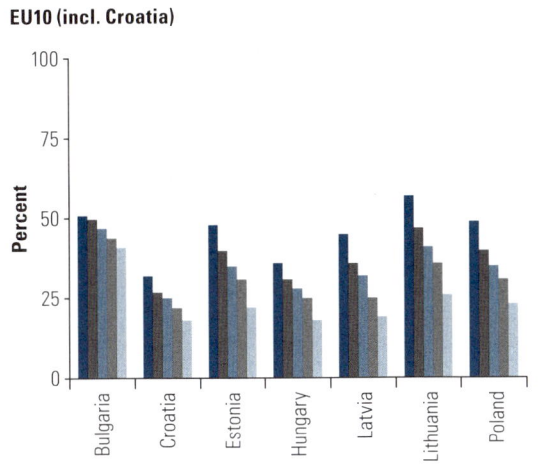

EU10 (incl. Croatia)

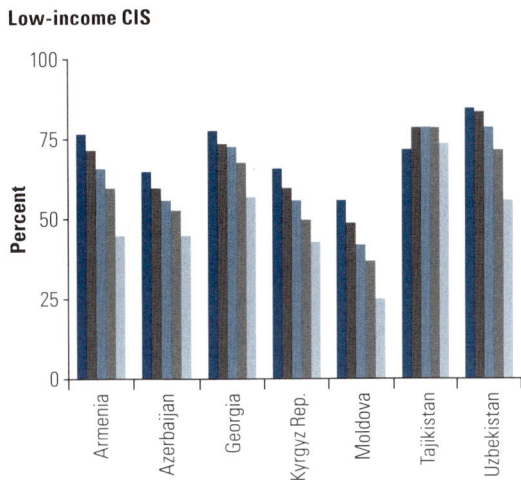

Low-income CIS

Middle-income CIS

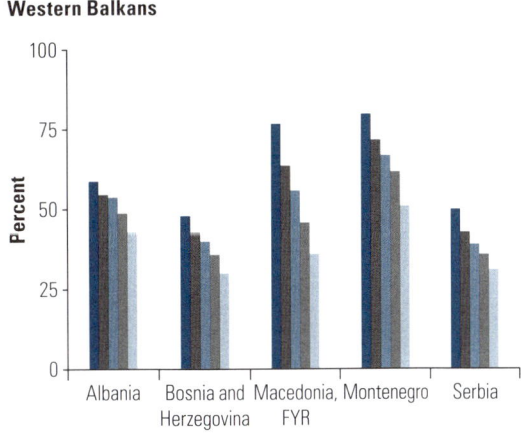

Western Balkans

Source: Staff calculations.

low-income CIS countries, food accounts for close to two-thirds of total consumption. In fact, across sub-regional groups, the average share of food consumption tracks the level of development fairly well. There are of course some exceptions. Ukraine, for example, which ranks as a middle-income country, has food shares that are more or less comparable with some of the low-income CIS countries.[39]

Second, within countries, there are substantial variations across geographic space and by household income (appendix tables 4 and 5). In Moldova, for example, the food share of rural household consumption is close to 50 percent; among urban households, it is about a third. In Poland, food accounts for about 50 percent of consumption among households in the lowest quintile; among households in the lowest quintile, the food share of consumption is a little more than a fifth.

Third, the energy shares of consumption do not reflect clear patterns along country, income, or geographic lines. In part, this may be due to the use of an imperfect proxy for energy share

FIGURE 2.16
Utility/Energy Shares of Consumption
In percent of total consumption, by quintiles of household consumption

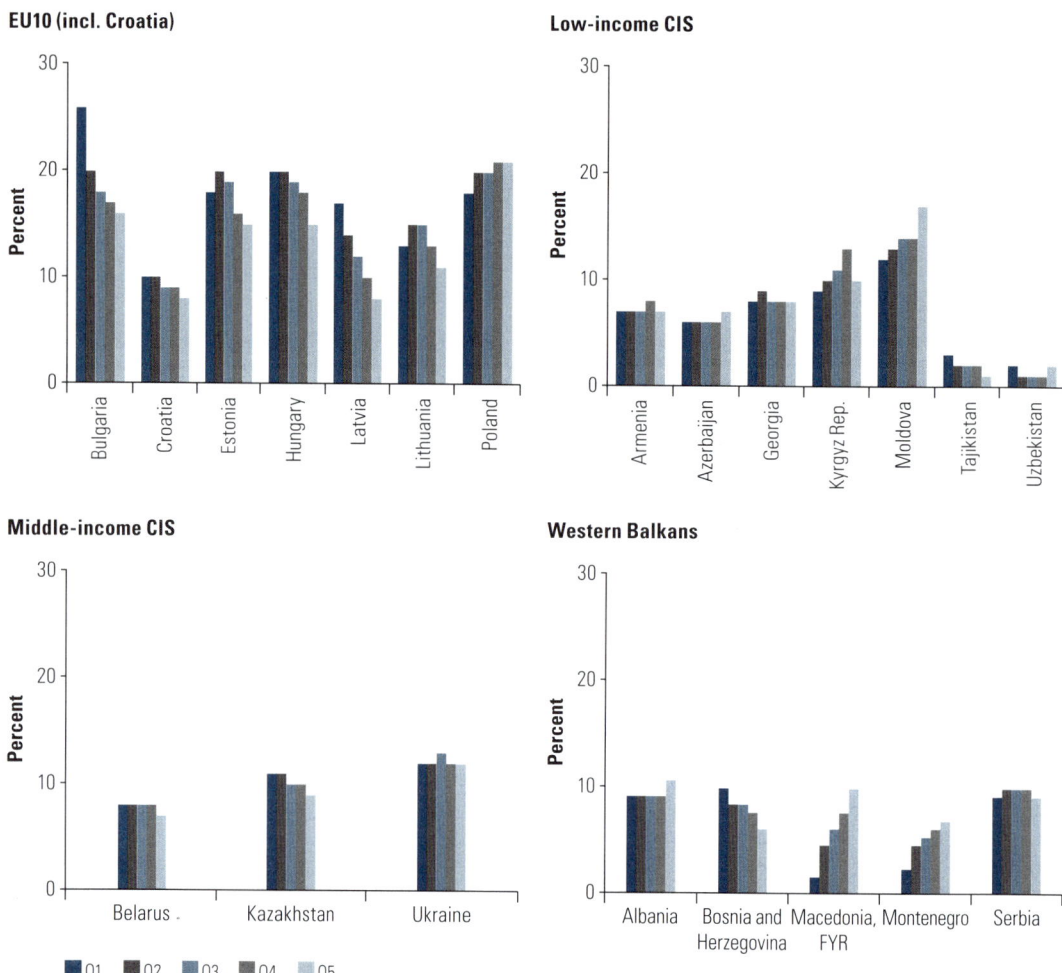

Source: Staff calculations.

of consumption. If the comparable consumption aggregates from the ECA Household Data Archives are used, the consumption component that comes closest to energy is the "utility" share of household consumption, consisting of expenditures on electricity, heat, gas, water, and sewerage. In addition, the state or quality of infrastructure matters as well. Where there is insufficient utility infrastructure, many households may not be connected to central sources of energy. In fact, in many countries, the utility shares of consumption among urban

households are somewhat higher compared to those of rural households. Furthermore, the expenditure shares could reflect non-payment or payment arrears. They could also possibly reflect access to less expensive sources of fuel and energy.

Aggregate energy shares of consumption also likely mask important variations across energy sources. Connection rates, intensity of consumption, and payment behavior, among others, are likely to vary across various energy sources, such as central heat, electricity, natural gas, and other sources of fuel. In Moldova, for example, households connected to central heating units are mostly urban households. In contrast, there is almost universal electricity connection.[40]

Some patterns in the utility shares of consumption may also reflect country-specific policies on utility tariffs, which can be lower than or equal to the relevant cost-recovery levels depending on whether utility reform programs have been completed. In fact, in countries known for energy tariffs that have not been completely adjusted to full cost-recovery, the utility shares of consumption are relatively low. The utility shares of consumption in Belarus and Ukraine, for example, are about half or even a third of utility shares among some of the new EU member states.

An analysis conducted by the World Bank in the middle of the crisis suggested that the welfare impacts of last year's food and fuel price increases were possibly very large. The study found that for some ECA countries, a 5 percent relative increase in food prices could worsen poverty ratesby up to 3 percentage points.[41]

One simple numerical exercise for assessing the welfare impact of illustrative food (or energy price) increases would be to calculate the fall in real income associated with these increases. This follows previous studies of fuel and food price increases, including selected ECA countries.[42] The calculations are made using two plausible scenarios. One scenario assumes no substitution while another scenario allows for a limited degree of substitution. The distribution of such welfare effects across all households can then be analyzed.

Previous studies thus essentially calculate two indexes of price change.[43] One index, the Laspeyres price index, assumes that consumption quantities in the baseline period are fixed. It does not allow for substitution toward cheaper alternatives. The other price index, the geometric price index, allows for some degree of substitution. An alternative way to interpret these calculations would be as compensations

needed to ensure that the households are as well off as they were prior to the price change or that household utility is kept constant. In the case of the Laspeyres index, this is consistent with the items and quantities of consumption remaining unchanged, with underlying preferences characterized by a Leontief utility function (i.e., no substitution). In the case of the geometric index of relative price change, it reflects Cobb-Douglas preferences and allows for substitution away from relatively more expensive goods but keeps household utility constant.

The welfare effects are of course proportional to the budget share of food consumption, by construction. The results are in the appendix (appendix tables 6 and 7). Across all countries in the region, the poor bear a greater burden of the welfare impact of a food price increase. The differences along geographic lines are also clear: rural households are hit harder compared to urban households. With respect to a 10 percent fuel price increase, the distributional consequences are less clear. In many countries, urban households and the more affluent households bear a greater burden of the welfare impact; this, however, is not true everywhere. Where there is some possibility of substitution, the welfare impact is smaller; this is true for both food and fuel price increases.

Country Illustrations

Within countries, there is likely to be substantial heterogeneity in the welfare impact of a price shock. The regional simulations above ignore a number of household specificities that determine the net poverty impact of food or energy price increases. As previously stated, the welfare impact of rising food price depends, in part, on whether households are net buyers or net sellers of food. The unfavorable consequences of rising prices can also be offset by rising real transfers or real wage increases. This section illustrates some of these dimensions drawing from countries where the food or fuel price increases that have taken place are among the sharpest in the region.

In the Kyrgyz Republic, for example, the food price increases are estimated to have had substantial welfare effects on net consumers.[44] Although the share of food in total consumption falls with income (and is thus highest among the poor, as we saw from the regional overview in the previous section), the share of net food consumers generally rises with income. However, net consumers still represent the majority of households in the poorest quintile. More generally, for the country as a whole, 53 percent of the population lives in households characterized as net food consumers. Of these net consumers, 35 percent are poor. As a result, about 19 percent of the population are net food consumers as well as living in poverty, and were estimated to have been hurt the most by the food price increases in 2007.

FIGURE 2.17

Kyrgyz Republic: Net Food Consumers and Net Food Producers
In percent of households

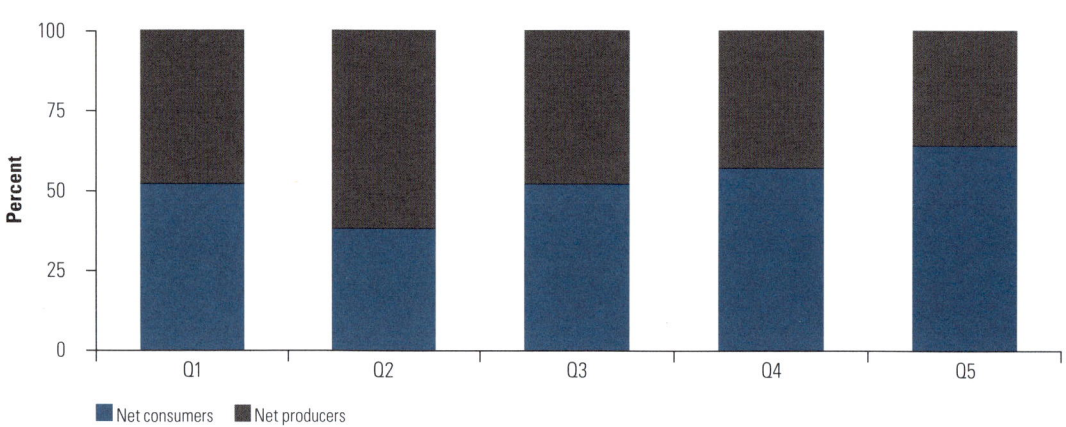

Source: Staff calculations.

FIGURE 2.18

Kyrgyz Republic: Estimated Poverty Impact of the Food Crisis
In percent of the populations

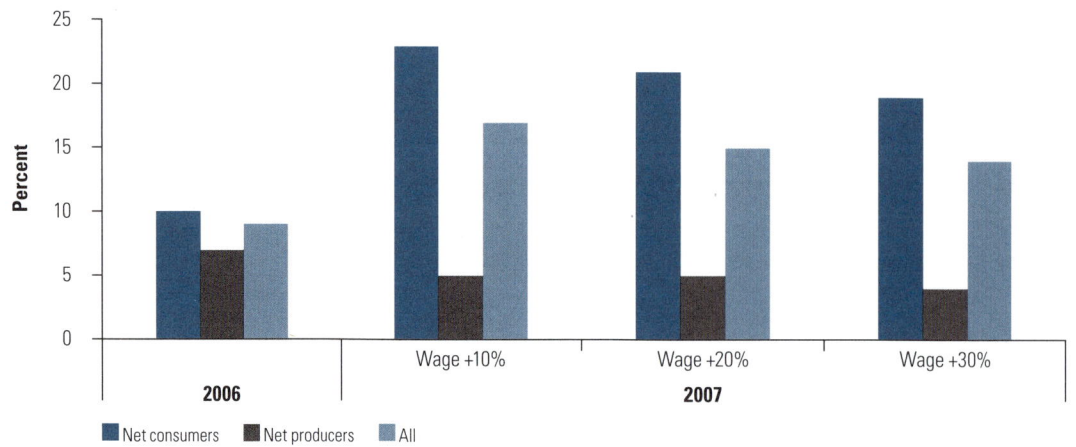

Source: Staff calculations.

At the same time, the welfare consequences of rising food prices were partially offset by rising wages in the Kyrgyz Republic. Not surprisingly, the estimated net impact on absolute poverty (with the poverty headcount at 40 percent in 2006) was inconclusive. Extreme poverty, however, was estimated to increase by up to 8 percentage points (from 9 percent in 2006), depending on the degree of wage increase. This percentage point increase is equivalent to about 400,000 people falling into extreme poverty because of rising food prices. Urban poverty was also estimated to increase. This is not surprising considering that about 30 percent of all net consumers live in the capital.

In Tajikistan and Albania, the net poverty impact is mediated by access to agriculture inputs, assets, and livelihood strategies. In a recent study of 11 countries, including

FIGURE 2.19
Albania: Welfare Impact by Livelihood
Bubbles represent the size of the population affected

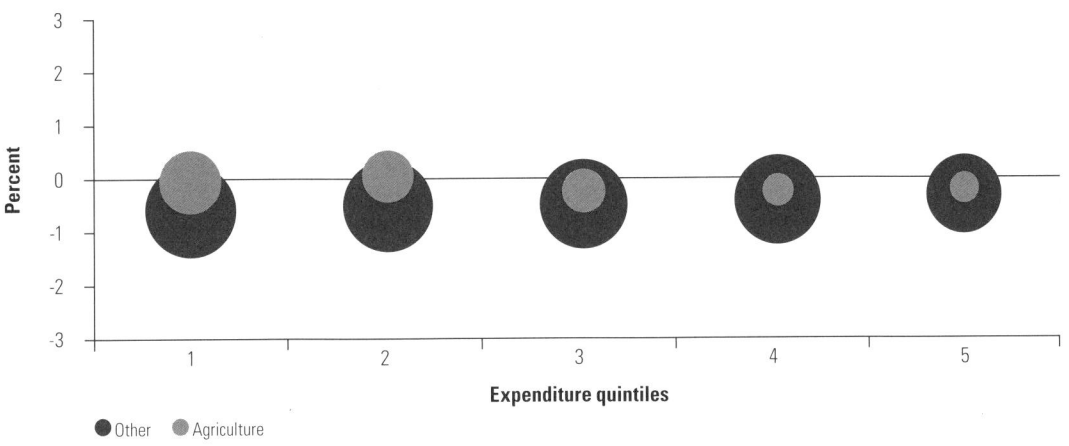

Source: Zezza et al. 2008.

FIGURE 2.20
Tajikistan: Welfare Impact by Livelihood
Bubbles represent the size of the population affected

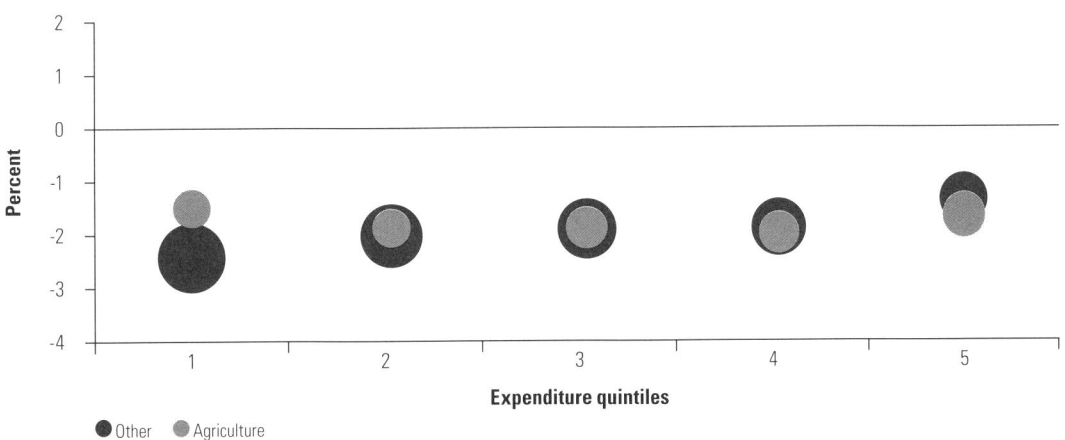

Source: Zezza et al. 2008.

Tajikistan and Albania, the authors found that the poorest households were likely to be hurt the most by food price shocks (figure 2.19 and figure 2.20).[45] They did find some evidence that some of the poor households manage to benefit from rising prices of basic commodities, depending on whether these households have sufficient access to agriculture inputs, or assets such as land.

Despite the moderating effects of livelihood and assets, the poor were nonetheless found to be the most likely to have been hit hardest by the price shock. This was true for all countries, irrespective of location within each country. This is not completely surprising, as the poorest households also have the weakest access to agriculture inputs and assets. They also tend to be relatively less educated, with relatively lower productivity and limited capability to take advantage of profitable activities in agriculture.

F.   Households and Income Shocks

Data and Methodology

This section follows the methodology underpinning recent simulations of the poverty implications of economic growth projections.[46] In brief, this section uses country-level projections for GDP and private consumption through 2010. Following existing exercises, we first assume that changes in GDP or income will not be passed on fully to private consumption. The impact will depend on the relationship between private consumption growth and GDP growth in each country. Next, the projected growth in private consumption is then used to predict per capita household consumption in each country, using the household survey data from the latest available year. Finally, the predicted household consumption is compared to the relevant poverty line.

The exercise yields two sets of results: (i) poverty projections using the pre-crisis GDP and private consumption projections and (ii) poverty projections calculated from more recent GDP and private consumption projections (released in January 2009 and April 2009). The difference between (i) and (ii) can be considered a measure of the poverty impact of the global crisis.

This section uses household survey data and macroeconomic growth projections. Household survey data are drawn from the ECA Household Data Archives. We have survey data for 25 of the 29 countries in the ECA region, representing 95 percent of the region's total population. Economic growth projections are drawn from the IMF's WEO database.[47] Growth projections at the country level are available for the pre-crisis period (April 2008) and for April 2009. The January 2009 WEO growth projections are available at the country level for some ECA countries (such as Russia); however, for most ECA countries, only sub-regional averages were made publicly available. These sub-regional averages were used to impute growth projections at the country level. Finally, we use historical data (covering the three years preceding the crisis) for each country to estimate the ratio between private consumption growth and GDP growth. On average, it is equal to one but there is some slight variation from country to country. (This assumption is discussed more fully below.) The underlying country data are reported in appendix table 8.

This numerical exercise uses a poverty line of $PPP 2.50 per person per day and a poverty/vulnerability line of $PPP 5.00 per person per day. This follows the most recent round of the International Comparison Program on purchasing power parities (PPPs). Although the World Bank recommends a new international poverty line of $PPP 1.25 per person, the $PPP 2.50 and $PPP 5.00 poverty/vulnerability lines have been found to be more relevant for ECA, to take into account the higher cost of living associated with the region's colder climate and the conditions in many middle-income countries throughout the region.[48] In addition, this follows the 2005 regional study that adjusted the region's international poverty line(s) to reflect similar considerations.[49]

Important Caveats[50]

These regional simulations are based on several strong assumptions, which are explained further below. Although these assumptions are defensible, there is a large, inconclusive literature on, among other things, whether these assumptions hold on average, whether they hold linearly or non-linearly (depending on, for example, the level financial sector development), and whether these assumptions hold depending on whether it is a "normal" period or a crisis period, and, during a crisis period, whether it is a financial crisis or a different kind of economic crisis.

These simulations ignore the distributional consequences of the crisis. The exercise assumes that the growth in per capita household consumption is distribution neutral; that is, households in every part of the income distribution are all affected uniformly by the average growth or decline in consumption. On one hand, previous research suggests that there has been no change in inequality, on average, during economic contractions, thus lending some support to this assumption. On the other hand, there may be disproportional effects on the poor depending on the relative exposure of households to the economic shock. In fact, despite the zero change in inequality on average, substantial variations exist from country to country.

A review of ECA's experience with previous crises suggests that, in fact, certain types of households tend to be more vulnerable during crisis periods.[51] For example, an analysis of vulnerability in Moldova reveals that the consumption of larger households experienced larger drops after the Russian financial crisis; moreover, controlling for household size (among other individual and household characteristics), the number of children in the household was associated with larger consumption

losses. Similar results were found in an analysis of Russian households over this same period: The more children are present in a household, the greater this household's poverty risk and the lower its ability to smooth consumption. In addition, households with higher initial incomes and more assets were found to be better able to protect their welfare during and after a macroeconomic shock, in large part due to their broader menu options of coping with the shock, such as by drawing from their savings or asset liquidation.

The exercise does not assume a unitary pass-through from GDP growth to private consumption growth as the economy contracts.[52] These simulations are based on the estimated ratio of private consumption growth to GDP growth using non-crisis data at the country level, which may be higher or lower than one, depending on actual country outcomes. However, there is no reason to think that this recent relationship will continue to hold over the crisis period.

A large literature has emerged on the relationship between consumption growth and GDP growth. In particular, the literature has explored what is typically referred to as "excess private consumption volatility" (relative to GDP or income growth volatility) and its possible drivers, including financial intermediation.[53] The literature postulates that financial deepening curbs consumption volatility, as financial markets promote risk sharing and allow households to smooth consumption. Some empirical studies have provided some supporting evidence, but they have also found this relationship to be nonlinear, requiring some sufficient level of financial deepening before yielding any measurable relationship between consumption smoothing and financial intermediation.[54] In addition, some recent studies of the fall in consumption during financial crises suggest that financial intermediation may exacerbate the decline in consumption, as consumption becomes more sensitive to the availability of bank credit.[55]

The regional simulations based on GDP shocks abstract from the potential household income shocks arising from reduced remittances due to the impact of the crisis in migrant host countries. As highlighted in the previous chapter, many countries in ECA are heavily dependent upon remittances as a source of foreign finance at the macro level. At the household level, such inflows can be important sources of funds for consumption expenditures, health and education, and investment. For example, in Tajikistan in 2007 around 60 percent of the yearly consumption of the median household was financed by remittances (World Bank 2009c). As outlined in the country studies detailed below, it is thus important to tailor the specific income shocks to country characteristics.

These simulations also ignore the many non-monetary and nonincome dimensions of poverty likely resulting from the crisis. As has been seen in previous crises, the social consequences of crises can be significant, as households cut back on their health care spending, pull children out of school, and curb many other essential expenditures.[56] Such social consequences may have immediate consequences, as well as longer-term implications for human capital formation, the intergenerational transmission of poverty, and the sustainability of long-term economic growth.

The results presented below for the region as a whole should thus be interpreted with caution. They should be treated as illustrative, taking into account many of the limitations of the calculations behind them. In some cases, the poverty impact may be understated, such as in the event that consumption substantially lags behind GDP growth in 2010. In other cases, the poverty impact may be overstated, where there are opportunities for consumption-smoothing and offsetting income shocks.

Regional Overview: Main Results

The results suggest that poverty will rise. By 2010, the poverty headcount (using the $PPP 2.5 poverty line) for the region as a whole is expected to be about 2.4 percentage points higher than it would have been, relative to baseline projections of income or GDP growth (figure 2.21). The share of the poor or vulnerable population also rises by 7.2 percentage points. In 2009, these shares rise by 1.6 and 5.9 percentage points, respectively. In absolute

FIGURE 2.21

The Impact of the Crisis on Poverty and Vulnerability in the ECA Region

Poverty and vulnerability projections 2007–2010, in percent of the population

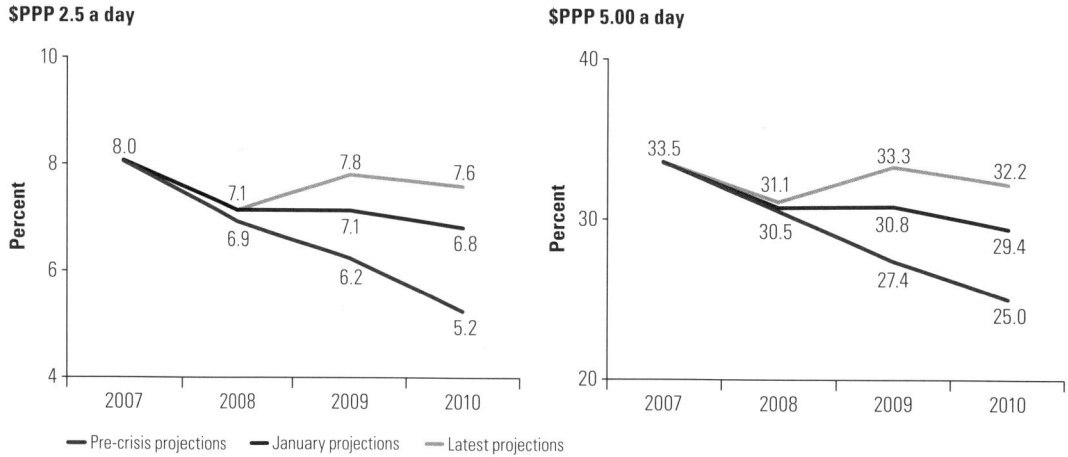

Source: Staff calculations.

terms, an additional 11 million people will fall into poverty by 2010. An additional 23 million people will find themselves vulnerable because of the crisis.[57] In 2009, 7 million more people are in poverty and 28 million more are either poor or vulnerable.

Turkey and the middle-income CIS countries are driving the percentage point increases in poverty and vulnerability, followed closely by the EU10 plus Croatia. Relative to baseline projections, the share of the poor and vulnerable population rises by over 8 percentage points, on average, in these countries. The relative

differences across sub-regions reflect the significant revisions to GDP growth projections (figure 2.22). Many of the middle-income CIS countries, for example, have experienced substantial downward revisions in their economic growth prospects between April 2008 and April 2009, with growth prospects switching from expansion to recession. Russia's 2009 growth projections, for example, fell from +6.8 to –6.5. Ukraine's growth prospects in 2009 declined from +4.9 to –7.3. In contrast, a number of low-income CIS countries still expect their economies to expand by modest amounts in 2009.

FIGURE 2.22

The Impact of the Crisis on Poverty and Vulnerability in the ECA Region: Sub-Regional Results

Poverty and vulnerability projections 2007–10, in percent of the population

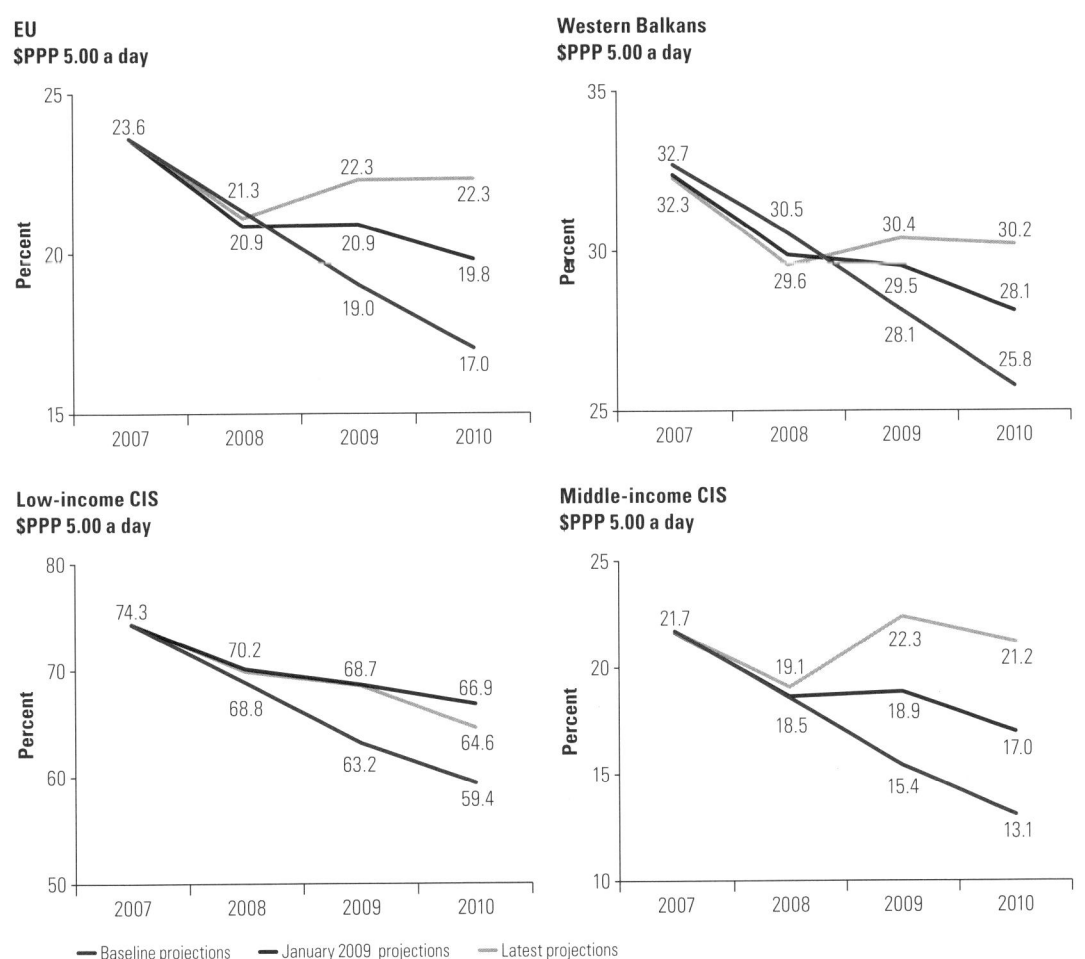

Source: Staff calculations.

These include Azerbaijan (+1.7), Georgia (+1.0), Tajikistan (+1.4), and Uzbekistan (+4.9), though all their GDP growth numbers have been revised downward as well. At the lowest end of these adjustments is Uzbekistan, with 2009 GDP growth numbers essentially unchanged from the pre-crisis period to April 2009.

Some Sensitivity Tests

The core simulations are based on the historical relationship between GDP growth and private consumption. We re-ran the simulations above to allow for a unitary pass-through from GDP growth to private consumption (and thus to household consumption). The key results are essentially unchanged—both for the region as a whole and for the sub-regions. Selected figures are presented in appendix figure 1.

The simulations were also re-calculated using the elasticity of poverty to growth in consumption per capita calculated for ECA countries over the period 1998–2003.[58] Because the period refers to the economic recovery period following the Russian crisis, the poverty elasticity estimates may not be appropriate. Nonetheless, the results are essentially unchanged.

Country Illustrations

The regional overview masks the likely heterogeneity of impact within countries. This regional analysis should not be a substitute for country-specific poverty analysis. As previously discussed, the results of the preceding numerical exercises ignore many country specificities and the likely concentration of vulnerable households, depending on the nature of the economic downturn. In addition, while some economies are still projected to grow by modest amounts, the welfare risks are not shared uniformly across all households.

Tajikistan is a case in point.[59] While the country as a whole is still projected to grow by a very modest amount through 2009, many households are vulnerable to falling demand

for foreign labor in Russia and Kazakhstan. As mentioned in Chapter 1, the growth of remittance outflows from Russia to CIS countries contracted in Q4 2008, tracking the declines in Russian construction activity. The latest figures indicate that the dollar value of recorded remittances to Tajikistan (via money transfers) fell 36 percent year-on-year in the first five months of 2009, with similar contractions seen in the heavily remittance-dependent economies of Georgia and Moldova. In Tajikistan the results of simulating the impact of up to a 50 percent fall in remittances suggest that the poverty headcount can rise by up to 7 percentage points, assuming households do not adjust (e.g., returning migrants do not find jobs in local labor markets), or by 3.5 percentage points, allowing for some adjustment on the part of households.

In Armenia,[60] the poverty headcount is estimated to increase by over 5 percentage points between 2008 and 2010, primarily driven by shocks transmitted through labor market channels. Many will find themselves out of work or earning substantially less than in previous years, particularly in sectors such as the construction and mining sectors. In addition, the impact on remittance-dependent households could be large. The results of recent analysis suggest that the poverty headcount may rise from 18 percent to 27 percent in households that receive remittances from sources other than immediate family members (a peculiar feature of household well-being in Armenia is the large share of remittances from non-immediate family members).

In Bulgaria,[61] the economic slowdown and the fall in remittances is estimated to lead to a 1.2 percentage point increase in poverty. Although more modest than the expected impact in other countries, the labor market is again an important transmission channel, particularly among workers in the construction sector. Declining remittances underpin about a quarter of the overall poverty increase, and a much larger share of the rise in extreme poverty.

In Russia,[62] the results of recent simulations suggest that the poverty headcount in rural areas will likely rise by over 5 percentage points. The simulations suggest that in addition to rural households, households with children and pensioners are at the highest risk of falling into poverty. The growth in unemployment levels will also drive increases in poverty.

Coping with the Crisis

A. Introduction

The resilience of households to macroeconomic shocks ultimately depends upon the economy's institutional readiness, the flexibility of the economic policy regime, and the ability of the population to adjust. Policy and institutional preparedness is essential so that countries can manage the adverse social impacts of macroeconomic shocks. This requires ex ante analysis of risks, a good understanding of their possible transmission channels if triggered, and their possible impacts on households; approaches that ensure that the state does not intervene excessively in terms of detrimental longer-term distortions to incentives or fiscal sustainability; and a comprehensive social safety net system that provides for countercyclical and scalable interventions.

This chapter looks at how the impact of the various shocks arising from the crisis on household welfare may be offset by households' own coping strategies and by social safety net systems. It will also assess some key constraints in the policy response to the crisis, drawing from some recent analyses of fiscal space and the availability of fiscal resources and a recent assessment of the performance of social protection programs in ECA countries. Finally, it will provide examples of possible policy responses to mitigate the impact of the crisis, by type of shock to households. The options for policy responses covered here are by no means exhaustive. They are discussed below mainly for illustrative purposes.

B. Household Responses: Lessons from the ECA Experience

Over the transition period, a growing literature has documented patterns of self-insurance, informal insurance, and informal risk pooling in ECA. They have also chronicled household strategies for coping with economic shocks, including borrowing, migration, substitution of consumption toward less expensive goods, and engaging in risky or illegal activities. Such strategies and risk mitigation mechanisms may be disproportionately concentrated among certain groups of households, depending on their region of residence, income, and social capital.

Households in ECA have employed a variety of coping strategies to smooth consumption during previous crisis periods. Some of these strategies correspond to what is referred to in the literature as "risk management."[63] These include household members holding jobs with uncorrelated risks, either domestically or through migration of family members to foreign countries. Other strategies, such as dissaving, including asset liquidation, and borrowing where possible, smooth consumption over time and still other strategies share risks across households (inter-household private transfers). Generally, the empirical literature rejects the existence of full consumption insurance, whereby temporary income fluctuations have no effect on consumption, but does provide some support to partial consumption smoothing, whereby consumption changes are smaller than income changes. This implies that, in general, households in the region were successful, albeit only partially, in protecting their welfare through crisis times by relying on a variety of coping strategies as described in more detail below.[64]

Labor supply adjustments. In response to falling income due to the effects of a macroeconomic shock, a household can increase its involvement in the labor market. Those already employed can increase their hours worked, or find secondary employment. Other members of the household can transition out of inactivity in order to supplement household income. Existing studies of Bulgaria, Russia, and Turkey indicate that, in general, labor supply adjustments have not allowed households in the ECA region to preserve their pre-crisis welfare levels. The proportion of households that found secondary employment is small and the earnings were generally insufficient to compensate for the loss of income from primary jobs.

Migration. As local employment opportunities decline, one option would be to relocate to a region with better labor market conditions. Labor migration can be internal or international, and it can involve either the whole household or only some of its working-age members. The necessary conditions for the effectiveness of this coping strategy are labor market flexibility and the ability and willingness of workers to move to locations with jobs plus a host region likely to provide sufficient labor income gains to offset migration costs. In the years following the Russian crisis, for example, many Moldovans migrated abroad in search of employment opportunities and better living conditions. Studies of household behavior during the early transition period in Kazakhstan also found that migration responded almost immediately to movements in relative exchange rates and to systemic crises, such as the 1998 Russian financial crisis. However, wage differentials and differences in construction activity have been found to take a longer time in influencing migration patterns. A recent study of Turkey found that rural-to-urban migration has been the most important informal coping strategy, leading to increased urbanization in all regions of Turkey. The broad-based nature of the ongoing downturn, affecting both traditional host and source countries, is clearly an important determinant of the effectiveness of this coping strategy in the current economic environment.

Subsistence Farming. Households that have access to private land plots can use them to supplement their income by selling the home-produced goods or to augment their own consumption with such home production. Studies of household behavior in Bulgaria, Russia, and Turkey during previous crises observe that subsistence farming has often been employed by households to supplement their food consumption. However, it has also been found to be an ineffective coping strategy to address vulnerabilities in non-food consumption, or in lifting households out of poverty.

Dissaving/Borrowing and Asset Liquidation. By saving a portion of its income flow in good times and dissaving (or borrowing) in bad times, a household can minimize consumption variability in the presence of income fluctuations. The same principle applies to the accumulation of assets (such as housing, durables, production equipment) in good times and the sale of such assets in bad times. Of course, the usefulness of this strategy depends on households' access to credit markets and their ability to dispose of their assets after a macroeconomic shock. For example, many households in Turkey turned to selling their assets during the 2001 crisis. About 20 percent of households reported selling assets and valuables. However, it has also been suggested that proceeds from such asset sales were meager due to insufficient demand for assets held by the poor. This is similar to the phenomenon of asset "fire-sales" in financial markets potentially yielding prices below fundamental values (and a wealth redistribution from net sellers to buyers). In addition, as highlighted in the discussion of household indebtedness, household gross asset positions may be associated with financial liabilities such as mortgages, thus limiting the potential net gains from such sales (or even leading to potential net losses as in the case of negative mortgage equity).

Private transfers. Besides turning to the government for assistance, households suffering from the impacts of an economic shock can turn for help to friends and family. If the shock does not affect households equally—that is, more technically, if the idiosyncratic component of the economic shock is large compared to the covariate component—then households can reduce consumption volatility through inter-household transfers, flowing from less affected households to more affected households. In ECA, private transfers have been found to be an important buffer against household income and consumption volatility. However, macroeconomic crises decrease the likelihood that a household will be able to use this strategy effectively, since a widespread shock would, by definition, affect most people in that household's social network. Moreover, some marginalized groups, such as ethnic minorities, are often excluded from the informal support networks available to other households.

Compared to previous crises, the scope for households to engage in their traditional coping strategies may be more limited. During previous crises, households found secondary employment, relied on transfers from friends and families, or left for work abroad to augment family income. Because of the global nature of the crisis, and because macroeconomic shocks are hitting households on multiple fronts, these coping strategies may no longer be feasible.

For the poorest households, subsistence farming may be a viable strategy, though evidence from the recent food price shock suggests that many of the poorest households do not have access to agricultural assets and inputs. For some, transitions into informal sector employment may be possible though, for many households, earnings from informal sector activity will likely be insufficient to offset the poverty impact of the crisis.

C.   Context: Policy Response, Government Resources, and Constraints

Overall Fiscal Envelope

The ability of many governments in ECA to respond to the crisis—such as by increasing social transfers—is generally constrained by rising government deficits. Between 2007 and 2009, on average, deficits in percent of GDP are projected to rise by about 3 percentage points. There are marked variations across countries, with Estonia, Montenegro, and Russia at the higher end of this distribution, while Belarus, Hungary, and Georgia are at the lower end of the distribution. Nonetheless, for many countries, fiscal policy responses to the crisis will likely be muted by rising deficits that have become much more difficult to finance. It would be essential to first determine the overall fiscal adjustment warranted for macroeconomic stability and debt sustainability, taking into account initial conditions and the likely impact of the crisis on public finances.[65] Economies that experienced strong initial fiscal and external positions are likely to have more room for expansionary fiscal policy and can afford a fiscal stimulus package, while those with weaker initial positions may require substantial fiscal adjustment. Other features of a country's macroeconomic policies are also important. For example, countries with fixed exchange rates will have to depend more on fiscal policy, rather than monetary policy, for adjustment.

A recent analysis in fact suggests that there are likely large shortfalls in education and health spending worldwide due to the growth slowdown.[66] ECA countries, as a group, will require the largest outlays, compared with other regions, to protect their planned expenditures in education and health services. With regard to relative fiscal constraints, ECA is in a better position. However, there is still potentially a large shortfall in education and health spending among countries with little fiscal capacity and it is not likely to be financed by donor resources.

Where there are no new official or alternative sources of financing, or where there is little scope to mobilize revenues, some countries may resort to across-the-board cuts in public spending.[67] Although social safety nets will be among those items likely to be cut as revenues fall, protecting these programs—and possibly expanding some of them, where some reallocation of resources is possible—will be an important element in the response to the crisis.

The prioritization of labor-using investment expenditures—either from countries' own budgets or from resources provided by donors—could be one option for addressing the labor market consequences of the crisis while accounting for constrained fiscal resources. Such investments could include rural roads projects or irrigation systems rehabilitation

FIGURE 3.1

General Government Balances in ECA, 2007 and 2009

In percent of GDP

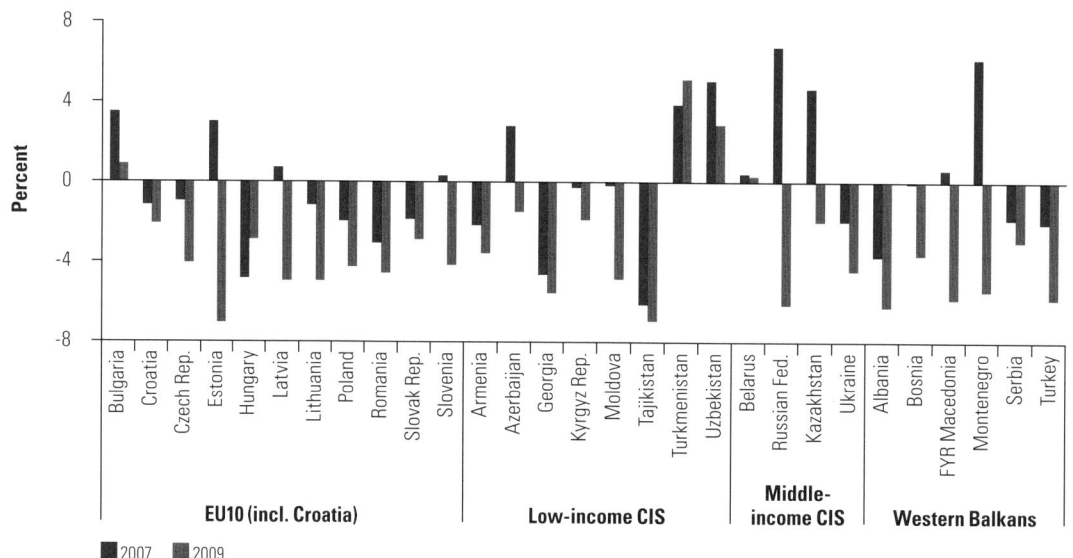

Source: IMF WEO database (April 2009).

projects that can create short-term employment opportunities while creating the conditions for longer-term growth. Improving the efficiency of public spending may also create some additional fiscal space.

Existing Social Protection Systems[68]

Countries in the region operate a combination of safety net programs. The programs are typically in the form of cash transfers with an emphasis on family allowances (such as child allowances), social pensions, heating and housing allowances, and targeted anti-poverty programs. Some countries in ECA have yet to reform a range of categorical benefits and subsidies left over from the pre-transition period. Across countries, multiple programs exist, leading to the fragmentation and duplication of benefits.

The region's social protection systems currently vary in size and targeting performance across countries. The results of comparing the targeting performance of selected social assistance benefits across countries suggest that Lithuania, Ukraine, and Turkey are among the countries with the bulk of social benefits reaching the poorest households. At the lower end are countries where only 40 percent of the social benefits reach the poorest quintile. However, most countries in the region have at least one targeted safety net program that can possibly be scaled-up in response to the crisis. Expanding such programs can take place either by increasing the value of benefits they provide or by expanding their coverage to reach those households still currently outside the system. However, in some countries, including Belarus, Bosnia, Hungary, Kazakhstan, Moldova, and Russia, the targeting performance of existing programs remains weak.

Depending on a country's initial conditions, the response to the crisis in terms of social assistance may involve expanding some well-performing programs, reforming relatively less effective interventions, or, alternatively, introducing new programs as appropriate. The experiences of other countries suggest that programs such as conditional cash transfers (CCTs),[69] workfare schemes, and public works programs can be effective instruments for protecting the vulnerable from immediate as well as longer-term (second-round) consequences of transitory shocks on nonincome dimensions of welfare, including human capital accumulation.

D. Immediate Policy Responses: Some Illustrations

This section provides illustrations of potential policy responses and instruments for mitigating the poverty and social impact of the crisis. The examples are organized by type of shock to households. The treatment of the topic is not comprehensive and the options listed are by no means exhaustive. The options are instead discussed below for illustrative purposes.

Across various policy instruments and social protection programs, there are a number of important considerations. The primary consideration would of course be the appropriate role for the government—whether the government responds to the crisis through expenditure policy, tax policy, or regulatory policy. Another important consideration would be the fiscal cost of a program, the administrative ease with which it can be implemented, and the incentives it creates. It will also be important to consider whether a program should have universal coverage, or whether it should be narrowly targeted or self-targeted. As explained below, country-specific resources and institutions will drive the relative merits of these instruments.

Credit Market Shocks

In countries where households are experiencing rising debt service burdens, governments may have to consider facilitating the restructuring of household debt in default.[70] In many ECA countries where banks currently have limited capital buffers, bank responses to rising nonperforming loans have focused on extending grace periods. However, without the certainty of a rapid economic recovery, these restructuring strategies effectively postpone problems into the near future. This creates substantial risks of under-provisioning and inadequate recognition of losses and thus of over-estimating bank solvency.

There is a role for governments to provide incentives for proper debt restructuring. Defining the right framework is challenging as it requires balancing competing pressures on banks, households, and the government in a way that is fiscally affordable, creates minimal market disruption, is socially acceptable, and allows banks to remain solvent and able to resume lending in the medium term.

A template for government-assisted household debt restructuring has been proposed recently.[71] The authors advocate a restructuring program that reflects some essential features including simplicity and limited scope, as well as participation on a voluntary basis, among other features. They consider two general approaches, one involving the creation of a legal and institutional framework that can underpin case-by-case debt restructuring. The other approach is based on some form of financial assistance by the government.

The estimated cost of providing financial assistance to indebted households at risk of default is relatively modest, on average, though with variations across countries. Simple calculations can be made for the cost of compensating indebted households who are subjected to an interest rate shock in Estonia, Hungary, and Lithuania and an exchange rate shock in Hungary and Ukraine. This is based on the assumption that *all* households are fully compensated for the increase in the debt service burden resulting from the shock. In Estonia, Hungary, and Lithuania, the implied costs of

an interest rate shock are 0.44, 0.19, and 0.17 percent of GDP, respectively, equivalent to about 29 percent, 6 percent, and 12 percent of the social assistance budget, respectively. In Hungary and Ukraine, the compensation for an exchange rate shock is 0.04 and 0.22 percent of GDP, respectively, equivalent to about 2 and 15 percent of the social assistance budget, respectively.[72] In general, these are relatively small sums, except in Estonia. The share of indebted households in these countries that is still not as large as those in more advanced economies likely drives this.

On the other hand, the fiscal cost of assisting severely indebted households may be an underestimate for a number of reasons. First, the SILC-based calculations (Estonia, Hungary, and Lithuania) include mortgage interest payments only, because SILC data allows us only to assess the rising cost of mortgage debt service. Taking all of household debt service costs together may then yield a much bigger sum. Second, the risk exposure varies by type of household debt. In Hungary, in particular, we know from central bank data that the exchange rate exposure of consumer loans is much larger than the exchange rate exposure of housing loans (60 percent versus 84 percent at the end of 2008). The SILC and Ukraine data are for 2007 and our calculations are based on households reporting themselves as indebted. Between 2007 and 2008, the pool of indebted households may have expanded further.

External Price Shocks

Increases in the domestic prices of energy and food pose both short- and long-term challenges for policymakers.[73] In the current environment, the short-run inflationary pass-through of higher imported food and energy prices, including those due to exchange rate effects, may be offset by falling domestic demand as economic activity weakens. However, managing inflation using appropriate policy instruments remains important. The full pass-through of price increases to consumers avoids introducing distortions into productive incentives, with support for vulnerable households to be provided by appropriate, well-targeted social assistance within the constraints imposed by a country's fiscal space. A country may also opt for a gradual phase-in of energy tariff adjustments, where the price increases required by adjustment toward full cost recovery may be too steep.

The ECA region's previous experience with energy tariff adjustments suggests that direct transfers or tariff-based subsidies can play an important role in protecting poor households.[74] There is ongoing debate on the comparative merits of direct transfers and tariff-based subsidies, such as a lifeline tariff or charging a lower tariff for an initial minimum level of energy consumption. Opponents of lifeline tariffs suggest that they are expensive and, for at least the initial block of, for example, electricity consumption, such lifeline tariffs subsidize both poor and nonpoor consumers alike. However, supporters of lifeline tariffs argue that where poverty is prevalent, where there is close to universal access to network energy, and where social transfers are not well targeted, there is a case to be made for tariff-based subsidies.

It is also important that policy responses do not conflict with the key longer-term reform agenda. For example, authorities should guard against reversal of efforts to lower quasi-fiscal deficits in the energy sector, which is an ongoing challenge in many ECA countries. It will also be critical to maintain an open and transparent trading regime. Although some countries within ECA adopted restrictive trade and price controls in response to the food price increases in 2007, many of them have now been reversed. For example, Ukraine eliminated its export quotas in June 2008 and Kazakhstan lifted its export ban in September 2008. At the same time, work needs to continue toward medium- to longer-term goals for improving the policy environment for agricultural productivity growth,

improving energy efficiency, and strengthening social safety nets and other risk mitigation systems. Finally, communication to the public of the policy choices adopted to address the impact of higher energy and food prices, and the various trade-offs which are involved, may help build broader constituencies in support of the adopted policies.

Income and Employment Shocks

The unemployment insurance system, the main tool for addressing rising unemployment, may not be sufficient to mitigate the impact of the crisis. In fact, the unemployment insurance system itself may suffer from several limitations, including weak incentives for reducing welfare dependency or for job search. Benefit durations are long and can be expensive. Moreover, none of the existing programs are available for returning migrant workers, for example due to a lack of work history necessary for unemployment insurance or a lack of permanent residence required for social assistance. This suggests that it may be worthwhile to consider alternative approaches to social protection.

More generally, the global crisis will probably create "the new poor," or households that may be among those in higher income quintiles in the pre-crisis period but made poor by shocks to their income flows, liabilities, or consumption. These households will likely not be reached immediately by existing social protection programs.

Public works programs were an important component of the overall safety net package in Argentina, Mexico, Korea, and Thailand during the so-called Tequila Crisis of 1995 and the 1997 East Asian crisis. Public workfare programs generally played an important role in mitigating the negative effects of the macroeconomic crises in these countries, though its relative role varied depending on the effects of the crisis on the labor market. With the exception of Mexico, income gains from public workfare programs were significant in these cases. For example, in Korea the main reason for launching a workfare program was the very sharp increase in unemployment, in both formal and informal sectors, because of the crisis. The rate of unemployment increased from about 2 percent prior to the crisis to 9.3 percent barely six months into the crisis. Not surprisingly, public works in Korea played a dominant role in providing immediate short-term employment opportunities at low wages. In contrast, in Mexico the labor market impact of the crisis was a dramatic fall in the real incomes of workers, with relatively more limited job losses. A cash income support program (*Progresa*) played a major role in social protection, with public works playing only a subsidiary role.

The ECA region's experience with workfare has been relatively limited. To date, simple, non-randomized evaluations are available for only four countries: Bulgaria, the Slovak Republic, Slovenia, and Poland.[75] These countries' experiences with workfare are summarized in Box 4.

A broader use of workfare in the region faces a number of constraints. First, workers in most countries in the region have access to unemployment insurance. Second, unemployment rates are quite high in some countries even during non-crisis periods. Third, most unemployed are long-term unemployed, with some looking for jobs for over two years, in contrast to many developing countries. Fourth, a uniform application of any policy across the region is not feasible given tremendous diversity within the region in terms of income, degree of urbanization, dependence on agriculture or manufacturing, and so on. Fifth, in many countries over a long period, there has been substantial emphasis on workers' rights, trade unions have been strong and influential, and the attitude toward a downward adjustment of wages has been generally hostile. By contrast, in more decentralized countries such as Argentina (and South Africa) there was less resistance to low wages, particularly

when communities are fully informed about program goals. Sixth, the term "public works" is often mistakenly associated with "forced labor." Indeed, in some countries the two terms have been used synonymously for years. Not surprisingly, workfare programs are not viewed favorably in the region. Finally, at the implementation level, it is common practice to use contractors. This creates its own problems, and requires careful attention to the tendering process and even greater attention to monitoring.

Given these constraints, what role can public works program play in ECA? With respect to the low-income countries in the region, public works program may have considerable merit. These countries have significant seasonal shortfalls in employment (during agricultural slack seasons). In addition, given very low yields of main agricultural crops, productivity-enhancing works, including the construction of rural infrastructure, have a role to play to promote agriculture productivity. Moreover, the design features of public works programs can be modified and adjusted relatively easily to suit this class of countries.

In contrast, the introduction of public works programs in the lower-middle- and upper-middle-income countries of the region requires more careful design and adjustment. For example, the central design feature of programs—the wage rate—needs to be set carefully, so that the level is higher than the unemployment benefit but lower than the prevailing market wage rate. In order for the program to be attractive to skilled and semi-skilled labor, projects need to be carefully selected to accommodate labor of varying skills, as was done, for example, in Korea.

The use of contractors to execute public works programs may pose a challenge, but there are suitable alternatives. In general, countries have followed two approaches: One option is to avoid using contractors at all (such as in Korea and Argentina) and let local governments and communities implement the program instead. Alternatively, a program can use contractors under a regulatory framework, which has taken several forms. For example, governments could fix the share of labor in each specific contract (say 30 percent wage cost in a road repair project) in the tendering process, and enforce it. Another option would be to provide a list of laborers in each locality that contractors could hire for any specific activity. Contractors provide a weekly report to the government on the number and names of persons working on a specific project, and the government will then transfer wages direct into the bank accounts of laborers. A third approach is to provide appropriate incentives in the tendering process: ask contractors to specify the share of labor cost in each project that they plan to execute, with the proviso that this would be one of the selection criteria. The chosen bid can then be the one that promises to meet quality standards and promises to use the highest labor share in total cost. This needs to be enforced and monitored on a weekly or monthly basis. In all of the above approaches, the government fixes the level of the wage and contractors have to follow accordingly. Clearly, in any of the above scenarios, contractors do not have the freedom to offer a wage that is different from the one fixed by the government.

Another difficulty could be market wages that are below the statutory minimum wage. Because governments cannot offer a wage less than the statutory minimum wage, this becomes a challenge. Argentina stated in its program document that what is provided is not a wage, technically, but compensation. However, contractors may refuse to offer a wage less than the minimum wage, even if the minimum wage were higher than the prevailing market wage.

Finally, contractors may bring in their own labor gangs to work on a project, instead of using local labor. To avoid this scenario, the appropriate requirements need to be specified clearly in the tender. In a depressed region with a high unemployment rate, contractors have to use available local labor, and only if such local labor is unavailable are contractors legally allowed to bring in labor from outside a region. This is not easy and tendering bids may be slower than otherwise. Clearly, if contractors are used, "self-selection" as a method of targeting may not be feasible and so other approaches to targeting need to be explored.

In sum, the following sequential decisions need to be taken: (i) Decide on whether a public works program is the right option. If so, what is the balance between public works and other programs already in place? (ii) When public works is chosen, decide on the specific design aspects critical for success for the chosen country. (iii) Decide on the implementation modalities. (iv) Finally, institute a credible monitoring and evaluation system. Regardless of which program is chosen, post-crisis settings require that full attention be paid to selecting the right targeting instrument to reach the intended groups, exploring possibilities for quickly scaling up the program throughout the country without compromising on the quality, and considering exit strategies upfront before launching any program.

E. Longer-Term Policy Responses

Over the longer term, there are various measures for limiting the risks borne by households as financial markets deepen. These include measures affecting both the demand- and supply-side of household financial products. In terms of the demand-side, promoting financial literacy may help households to understand the risks they expose themselves to because of their consumption, employment, borrowing, and asset portfolio choices. Addressing the supply-side dimension potentially incorporates a whole host of macro-financial policy measures.

Detailed examination of such measures is not within the scope of this report, but in its discussion of the generic policy implications of

BOX 4

Public Works Programs in ECA

Bulgaria. Bulgaria launched its public works program in 2002 in response to high long-term unemployment and a perceived heavy dependence of government beneficiaries on social assistance. The program aimed to promote a more "active" approach to social assistance. The benefit comprised a minimum monthly salary plus social insurance plus health insurance, but not unemployment insurance. Wages were set around 125 Leva (around $60) when the minimum wage was 110 Leva, but those employed had to give up social assistance benefits (40 Leva, on average, in 2002). The net wage cost of the program to the government was about 80 Leva per participant. Projects executed under the public works program included community infrastructure (construction and renovation), afforestation, and other environmentally useful tasks. Tripartite labor councils at the local and regional level selected project proposals based on bidding procedures. A training component was included, but few workers chose to participate. The long-term unemployed were given priority, and refusal to participate in workfare meant being dropped out of the social assistance beneficiary list. Several ministries are involved in its implementation. In 2003, 117,800 temporary jobs were created, and 79,400 persons were absorbed.

The program was recently evaluated[76] and several findings emerged. First, the program reduced unemployment spells among the long-term unemployed, thus preventing further deterioration of skills and work ethics. Second, by far the largest positive gain observed was with respect to self-confidence and job-search motivation. Third, completed projects and services were found to be of use to communities. One reason for the attractiveness of the program was that (eligible) participants received pensions, and all participants were covered by health insurance. At the same time, the program also suffered from many weaknesses. For example, only 8 percent of participants managed to get a job quickly in the private sector, mainly because of a lack of attention to training. Employers preferred those who underwent on-the-job training (only about 8 percent underwent such training). In addition, private firms and nongovernmental organizations (NGOs) that implemented public works were found to have trained their workers more compared to municipalities.

The *Slovak Republic* introduced public works in 1992, known as "socially purposeful jobs" (SPJ) and "publicly useful jobs" (PUJ). The two programs continued with some modifications through 1997–98. In the beginning, there was no emphasis on training but in 1997, both programs were reformed. Retraining was emphasized, and more attention was paid to targeting specific groups such as the disabled, long-term unemployed, young workers, and school leavers. SPJ and PUJ were then formally combined into a single program. Jobs were provided for workers of all skill levels. An assessment[77] of this program found that the vast majority of workers (90 percent of the total) had a higher transition rate to a regular job after participation in the program, although a few workers (10 percent of the total) had a lower transition rate. In general, female, lower educated, and older unemployed workers have had much greater difficulty in accessing regular jobs. The exit rate from PUJ jobs was quite high, mainly due to the positive effect of the retraining provided.

BOX 4 *(continued)*

Public Works Programs in ECA

Slovenia also introduced public works during 1992–96, in response to rising unemployment in the early 1990s. There was heavy reliance on public works, partly because of the limited success of other programs. The program consisted of creating jobs for the unemployed under the auspices of a public or a non-profit (NGO) organization. Projects were required to provide useful services or build infrastructure of use to communities. Jobs were for a period of one year. The objectives were to help workers maintain their workforce attachment and prevent the erosion of their human capital. The contractors (selected via a tendering process) organized and carried out public works as well as provided mentoring and training as needed. In comparison with programs in Hungary and Poland, Slovenian public works attracted significantly more educated participants and younger workers, and the program was more innovative. An assessment[78] concluded that Slovenian public works participants immediately found a job upon completing the program.

Poland implemented active labor market programs (ALMP) consisting of training and retraining and programs to enhance human capital, along with public works. A systematic evaluation of Polish ALMP showed training and retraining performed well, with the post-treatment employment rates of both female and male participants observed to be higher than those who did not participate in the program. By contrast, the public works program suffered from major distortions, mainly because of "benefit churning" and lack of attention to proper calibration of various benefits (unemployment compensation) and wage levels. In addition, program officials felt male heads of households deserved sustained income support, which in turn adversely affected the functioning of the public works program.[79]

Some important lessons emerge from the Polish experience. First, greater emphasis should have been given to the training of the long-term unemployed while they were employed in public works. Second, the careful monitoring of employer behavior should have been incorporated into the program, to curb abuses of hiring cheap labor under the program. Third, distortions in the functioning of programs should have been minimized by carefully calibrating program benefits (wage levels) with other benefits such as unemployment compensation.

household credit growth in emerging market countries, the IMF highlighted five key policy areas that can help to limit related financial stability risks.[80] These include prudent macroeconomic management to minimize the potential future likelihood of interest rate, exchange rate, and income shocks to households. The second set of measures relates to the usage of macro-prudential norms, such as on loan-to-value or debt-service-to-income ratios. The third area concerns improvements to the overall legal environment and infrastructure, such as in sharing credit information and effective enforcement of collateral. The fourth area relates to enhanced data availability on the risks in household credit portfolios both in aggregate and individually. Finally, as highlighted in the various trade-offs discussed throughout this report, authorities should recognize the potential impact on households of traditional economic management policy measures, such as exchange rate and interest rate adjustments.

Many of these generic policy messages have clear resonance for countries within

ECA. For example, while a number of countries within the EU10 have taken measures to limit the extent of foreign currency borrowing by households, a recent analysis found that they might have had only limited effects.[81] In particular, the analysis finds that while such measures appeared to influence the extent of foreign currency credit channeled through the domestic financial system, they may have had the effect of shifting borrowing toward nonresident financial institutions. This highlights the need to adopt a combination of policies, at both the macro-financial and household levels, to help mitigate the potential risks associated with increased household credit growth, for example relating to foreign currency or variable interest rate loans. The exact combination of policy measures that is appropriate to allow for the benefits of household credit growth while limiting the potential associated risks will depend on country circumstances.

Diversified sources of economic growth will also be critical in helping dampen ECA countries' vulnerability to macroeconomic shocks. In some ECA countries, recent growth performance has been underpinned by economic activity concentrated in a few sectors, such as the housing sector, or income flows from some dominant source, such as migrant labor.

Monitoring systems are important. Guaranteeing that statistical monitoring systems are in place and that relevant household data are collected regularly and made available for analyses are important measures for ensuring that household vulnerabilities are understood in a timely manner. Such monitoring systems can also help identify households at risk and ensure that they can be reached by a country's social protection system. The monitoring of vulnerabilities could include risks in household credit portfolios, as discussed previously.

Appendix

TABLE A.1
Interest Rate Shock and Borrowers at Risk
Percentage change in share of borrowers at risk, in percent of indebted households

| | Interest Rate Shock | | | | | | | |
| | 20% Threshold | | | | 30% Threshold | | | |
	Historical	3 pp	5 pp	6 pp	Historical	3 pp	5 pp	6 pp
Estonia	16.80	11.06	17.95	22.35	12.02	6.76	12.45	13.61
	(0.03)	(0.03)	(0.03)	(0.04)	(0.03)	(0.02)	(0.03)	(0.03)
Hungary	5.70	7.62	11.82	12.75	3.25	4.93	8.71	10.12
	(0.04)	(0.05)	(0.06)	(0.06)	(0.03)	(0.04)	(0.05)	(0.06)
Lithuania	8.39	5.50	11.28	13.34	4.58	3.73	6.95	7.52
	(0.06)	(0.04)	(0.06)	(0.07)	(0.04)	(0.04)	(0.04)	(0.05)

Source: Staff calculations.
Note: Absolute errors in parentheses. "pp" stands for percentage points.

TABLE A.2

Economic Shocks and Borrowers at Risk

Percentage change in share of borrowers at risk in percent of indebted households

	Exchange Rate Shock			Unemployment Rate Shock					
				Probability Assignment			Random Assignment		
	Historical	25%	35%	Historical	10 pp	15 pp	Historical	10 pp	15 pp
Estonia	...	5.51	9.02	9.05	11.64	16.40	10.86	14.31	20.98
	...	(0.04)	(0.05)	(0.08)	(0.09)	(0.11)	(0.10)	(0.11)	(0.13)
Hungary	5.40	3.72	6.10	3.31	12.04	17.42	3.30	12.37	18.03
	(0.04)	(0.03)	(0.05)	(0.04)	(0.07)	(0.08)	(0.04)	(0.07)	(0.08)
Lithuania	...	1.89	4.31	5.76	4.29	6.70	8.68	6.64	10.16
	...	(0.05)	(0.10)	(0.14)	(0.12)	(0.15)	(0.17)	(0.15)	(0.18)

Source: Staff calculations.

Note: Absolute errors in parenthesis. 20% threshold is used. "pp" stands for percentage points.

TABLE A.3

Economic Shocks and Borrowers at Risk

Percentage change in share of borrowers at risk in percent of indebted households

	Exchange Rate Shock			Unemployment Rate Shock					
				Probability Assignment			Random Assignment		
	Historical	25%	35%	Historical	10 pp	15 pp	Historical	10 pp	15 pp
Belarus	0.12	0.11	0.19	0.21	2.68	3.81	0.26	3.47	5.39
(2008)	(0.00)	(0.00)	(0.00)	(0.00)	(0.01)	(0.01)	(0.00)	(0.02)	(0.02)
Kazakhstan	0.13	0.18	0.36	0.46	2.99	4.56	0.69	4.52	6.97
(2005)	(0.00)	(0.00)	(0.00)	(0.00)	(0.01)	(0.01)	(0.00)	(0.01)	(0.01)
Serbia	0.05	0.05	0.05	0.65	2.36	3.70	0.77	2.82	4.43
(2008)	(0.00)	(0.00)	(0.00)	(0.01)	(0.01)	(0.02)	(0.01)	(0.01)	(0.02)
Ukraine	0.52	0.20	0.34	1.12	3.86	5.66	1.19	4.09	6.26
(2007)	(0.00)	(0.00)	(0.00)	(0.01)	(0.01)	(0.01)	(0.01)	(0.01)	(0.02)

Source: Staff calculations.

Note: Absolute errors in parenthesis. "pp" stands for percentage points.

TABLE A.4
Food Share of Consumption
In percent of total consumption

Share of Food	Location			Consumption Quintiles				
	All	Rural	Urban	Q1	Q2	Q3	Q4	Q5
EU10 (including Croatia)								
Bulgaria	47	54	44	51	50	47	44	41
Croatia	25	28	22	32	27	25	22	18
Estonia	35	38	34	48	40	35	31	22
Hungary	28	31	26	36	31	28	25	18
Latvia	32	36	29	45	36	32	25	19
Lithuania	41	51	37	57	47	41	36	26
Poland	36	41	32	49	40	35	31	23
Low-income CIS								
Armenia	64	70	61	77	72	66	60	45
Azerbaijan	56	57	55	65	60	56	53	45
Georgia	70	80	61	78	74	73	68	57
Kyrgyz Republic	55	56	54	66	60	56	50	43
Moldova	42	48	33	56	49	42	37	25
Tajikistan	76	78	71	72	79	79	79	74
Uzbekistan	75	79	69	85	84	79	72	56
Middle-income CIS								
Belarus	32	34	30	35	33	32	30	27
Kazakhstan	46	52	42	55	50	47	43	35
Russian Federation	42	51	38	56	49	43	36	24
Ukraine	57	65	53	66	61	57	54	47
Turkey								
Turkey	36	43	32	51	40	35	30	24
Western Balkans								
Albania	52	55	48	59	55	54	49	43
Bosnia and Herzegovina	39	37	41	48	43	40	36	30
Macedonia, FYR	56	59	54	77	64	56	46	36
Montenegro	66	65	69	80	72	67	62	51
Serbia	40	43	37	50	43	39	36	31

Source: Staff calculations.

TABLE A.5
Utility/Energy Share of Consumption
In percent of total consumption

Share of Fuel	Location			Consumption Quintiles				
	All	Rural	Urban	Q1	Q2	Q3	Q4	Q5
EU10 (including Croatia)								
Bulgaria	19	18	20	26	20	18	17	16
Croatia	9	10	9	10	10	9	9	8
Estonia	17	13	20	18	20	19	16	15
Hungary	18	18	18	20	20	19	18	15
Latvia	12	9	14	17	14	12	10	8
Lithuania	13	10	15	13	15	15	13	11
Poland	20	17	22	18	20	20	21	21
Low-income CIS								
Armenia	7	6	8	7	7	7	8	7
Azerbaijan	6	7	6	6	6	6	6	7
Georgia	8	4	12	8	9	8	8	8
Kyrgyz Republic	11	11	11	9	10	11	13	10
Moldova	14	13	16	12	13	14	14	17
Tajikistan	2	2	1	3	2	2	2	1
Uzbekistan	1	1	2	2	1	1	1	2
Middle-income CIS								
Belarus	8	8	8	8	8	8	8	7
Kazakhstan	10	10	10	11	11	10	10	9
Russian Federation								
Ukraine	12	8	14	12	12	13	12	12
Turkey								
Turkey	12	11	12	10	12	12	13	12
Western Balkans								
Albania	12	11	14	12	12	12	12	14
Bosnia and Herzegovina	10	11	10	13	11	11	10	8
Macedonia, FYR	8	6	9	2	6	8	10	13
Montenegro	6	7	5	3	6	7	8	9
Serbia	13	11	14	12	13	13	13	12

Source: Staff calculations.

TABLE A.6
The Welfare Impact of a 10 Percent Food Price Increase

| | Laspeyres Price Index | | | | Geometric Price Index | | | |
| | Location | | Consumption Quintiles | | Location | | Consumption Quintiles | |
	Rural	Urban	Q1	Q5	Rural	Urban	Q1	Q5
EU10 (including Croatia)								
Bulgaria	5.38	4.37	5.06	4.08	5.26	4.26	4.94	3.97
Croatia	2.80	2.22	3.25	1.81	2.70	2.14	3.14	1.74
Estonia	3.76	3.40	4.83	2.20	3.65	3.29	4.71	2.12
Hungary	3.10	2.58	3.61	1.81	3.00	2.49	3.50	1.74
Latvia	3.65	2.93	4.50	1.91	3.54	2.83	4.38	1.84
Lithuania	5.06	3.68	5.67	2.57	4.94	3.57	5.56	2.48
Poland	4.10	3.22	4.91	2.28	3.99	3.11	4.79	2.20
Low-income CIS								
Armenia	6.98	6.11	7.65	4.49	6.88	6.00	7.57	4.37
Azerbaijan	5.69	5.47	6.48	4.52	5.57	5.35	6.37	4.40
Georgia	7.99	6.13	7.79	5.67	7.92	6.01	7.71	5.55
Kyrgyz Republic	5.59	5.37	6.61	4.32	5.47	5.25	6.51	4.21
Moldova	4.84	3.34	5.64	2.53	4.72	3.23	5.52	2.44
Tajikistan	7.83	7.14	7.19	7.44	7.74	7.04	7.09	7.35
Uzbekistan	7.87	6.92	8.53	5.56	7.79	6.81	8.47	5.44
Middle-income CIS								
Belarus	3.40	3.04	3.54	2.70	3.29	2.94	3.44	2.61
Kazakhstan	5.17	4.18	5.46	3.53	5.05	4.07	5.35	3.42
Russian Federation	5.07	3.82	5.61	2.37	4.95	3.71	5.49	2.29
Ukraine	6.54	5.33	6.62	4.73	6.43	5.21	6.51	4.61
Turkey								
Turkey	4.30	3.18	5.11	2.38	4.18	3.08	4.99	2.29
Western Balkans								
Albania	5.53	4.79	5.89	4.29	5.41	4.67	5.78	4.17
Bosnia and Herzegovina	3.67	4.14	4.76	3.05	3.56	4.02	4.65	2.95
Macedonia, FYR	5.94	5.38	7.69	3.57	5.82	5.26	7.60	3.46
Montenegro	6.47	6.88	7.99	5.06	6.36	6.77	7.91	4.95
Serbia	4.33	3.74	5.03	3.12	4.21	3.63	4.91	3.01

Source: Staff calculations.

TABLE A.7

The Welfare Impact of a 10 Percent Fuel Price Increase

| | Laspeyres Price Index | | | | Geometric Price Index | | | |
| | Location | | Consumption Quintiles | | Location | | Consumption Quintiles | |
	Rural	Urban	Q1	Q5	Rural	Urban	Q1	Q5
EU10 (including Croatia)								
Bulgaria	1.8	2.0	2.6	1.6	1.73	1.91	2.47	1.57
Croatia	1.0	0.9	1.0	0.8	0.93	0.85	0.99	0.75
Estonia	1.3	2.0	1.8	1.5	1.28	1.90	1.69	1.42
Hungary	1.8	1.8	2.0	1.5	1.75	1.78	1.90	1.46
Latvia	0.9	1.4	1.7	0.8	0.87	1.33	1.66	0.74
Lithuania	1.0	1.5	1.3	1.1	0.97	1.45	1.22	1.06
Poland	1.7	2.2	1.8	2.1	1.60	2.10	1.73	1.98
Low-income CIS								
Armenia	0.6	0.8	0.7	0.7	0.55	0.77	0.68	0.64
Azerbaijan	0.7	0.6	0.6	0.7	0.63	0.59	0.57	0.65
Georgia	0.4	1.2	0.8	0.8	0.38	1.14	0.81	0.73
Kyrgyz Republic	1.1	1.1	0.9	1.0	1.01	1.06	0.86	0.96
Moldova	1.3	1.6	1.2	1.7	1.22	1.58	1.19	1.62
Tajikistan	0.2	0.1	0.3	0.1	0.21	0.13	0.29	0.14
Uzbekistan	0.1	0.2	0.2	0.2	0.10	0.21	0.15	0.19
Middle-income CIS								
Belarus	0.8	0.8	0.8	0.7	0.72	0.74	0.74	0.71
Kazakhstan	1.0	1.0	1.1	0.9	0.97	0.97	1.05	0.85
Russian Federation	0.0	0.0	0.0	0.0				
Ukraine	0.8	1.4	1.2	1.2	0.80	1.37	1.16	1.18
Turkey								
Turkey	1.1	1.2	1.0	1.2	1.08	1.20	0.99	1.16
Western Balkans								
Albania	1.1	1.4	1.2	1.4	1.07	1.33	1.11	1.31
Bosnia and Herzegovina	1.1	1.0	1.3	0.8	1.07	0.95	1.25	0.75
Macedonia, FYR	0.6	0.9	0.2	1.3	0.59	0.82	0.18	1.22
Montenegro	0.7	0.5	0.3	0.9	0.66	0.51	0.28	0.85
Serbia	1.1	1.4	1.2	1.2	1.08	1.32	1.13	1.19

Source: Staff calculations.

TABLE A.8
Summary Data: GDP Growth and Poverty Simulations

Country	Baseline Poverty Headcount[1]		GDP Growth Projection for 2009		Estimated Growth in Per Capita Private Consumption for 2009	
	$PPP 2.5	$PPP 5.00	Baseline	Apr 2009	Baseline	Apr 2009
Albania	15.0	60.0	5.6	-0.1	6.0	-0.1
Armenia	30.0	84.0	5.6	-7.1	4.9	-6.2
Azerbaijan	1.0	71.0	14.7	1.7	10.6	1.2
Belarus	1.0	13.0	7.4	-3.4	6.9	-3.1
Bosnia and Herzegovina	1.3	8.0	4.6	-3.3	4.7	-3.3
Bulgaria	3.1	20.0	5.6	-1.3	5.9	-1.4
Croatia	0.0	2.0	4.0	-3.5	3.9	-3.5
Estonia	2.0	18.0	3.9	-10.1	4.0	-10.3
Georgia	39.0	76.0	9.8	1.0	10.8	1.1
Hungary	0.0	7.0	2.7	-3.2	2.8	-3.3
Kazakhstan	7.0	54.0	6.9	-2.1	7.3	-2.2
Kyrgyz Republic	52.1	88.1	6.9	-2.1	7.0	-2.1
Kosovo	38.1	82.0	5.7	-2.0	5.8	-2.0
Latvia	1.0	12.0	0.8	-11.7	0.8	-11.9
Macedonia	10.0	37.1	4.7	-2.3	4.9	-2.4
Moldova	30.0	77.0	8.0	-3.4	10.1	-4.3
Montenegro	10.2	49.2	5.7	-2.0	5.8	-2.0
Poland	2.0	20.0	4.7	-0.7	4.5	-0.7
Romania	7.0	45.0	5.1	-3.8	4.8	-3.6
Russian Federation	3.0	20.0	6.8	-5.6	7.7	-6.3
Serbia	2.0	17.1	5.7	-2.0	5.4	-1.9
Tajikistan	56.0	89.0	0.4	1.4	6.8	1.5
Turkey	15.0	49.0	3.1	-6.1	3.0	-6.0
Ukraine	1.0	18.0	4.9	-7.3	6.0	-8.9
Uzbekistan	19.0	67.0	5.4	4.9	5.5	5.0

Sources: ECA Regional Household Data Archives, IMF World Economic Outlook database, and staff calculations.

1   Latest year for which data are available.

FIGURE A.1

The Impact of the Crisis on Poverty and Vulnerability

Allowing for full pass-through from GDP growth to private consumption growth, in percent of the population

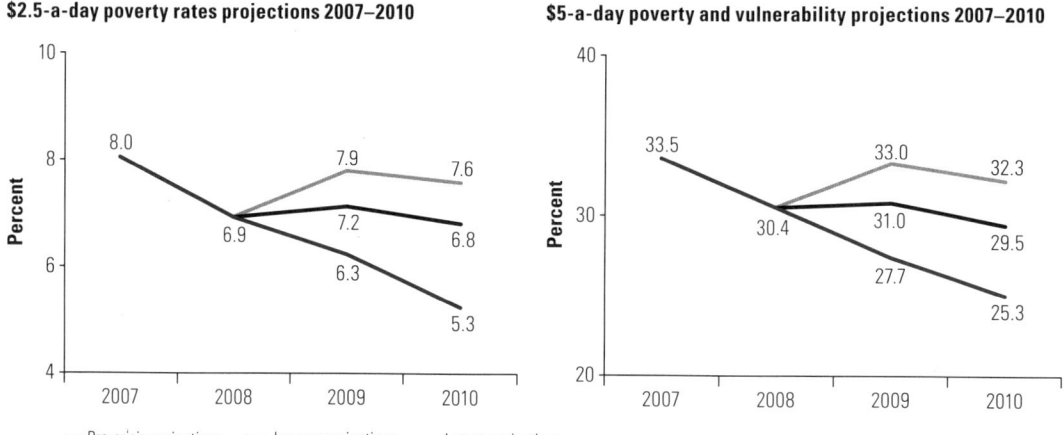

$2.5-a-day poverty rates projections 2007–2010

$5-a-day poverty and vulnerability projections 2007–2010

── Pre-crisis projections ── January projections ── Latest projections

Source: Staff calculations.

FIGURE A.2
Financial Margins in Selected Countries
Evidence from HBS Data, in local currency and in percent of all households, by years

Household vulnerability, Belarus
Cumulative distribution of household financial margins[1]

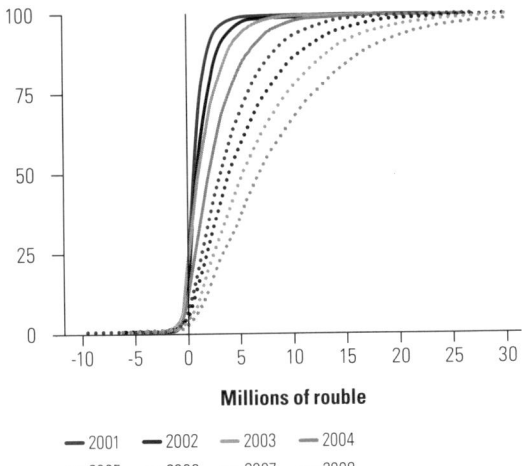

Millions of rouble

— 2001 — 2002 — 2003 — 2004
··· 2005 ··· 2006 ··· 2007 ··· 2008

Household vulnerability, Kazakhstan
Cumulative distribution of household economic margins[2]

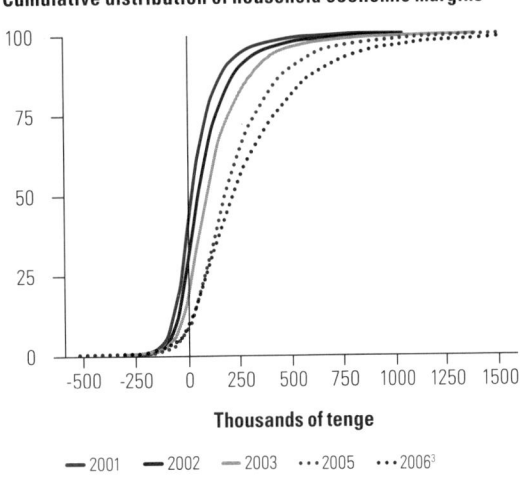

Thousands of tenge

— 2001 — 2002 — 2003 ··· 2005 ··· 2006[3]

Household vulnerability, Serbia
Cumulative distribution of household economic margins[4]

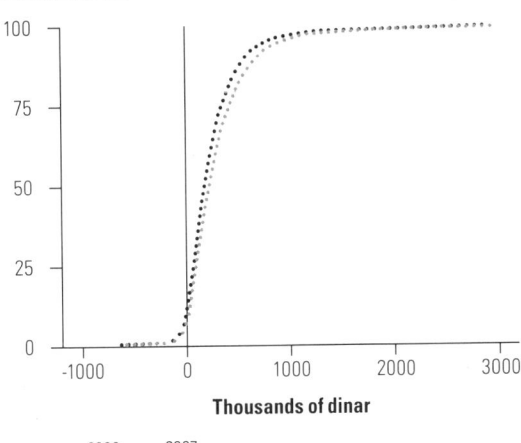

Thousands of dinar

··· 2006 ··· 2007

Household vulnerability, Ukraine
Cumulative distribution of household economic margins[5]

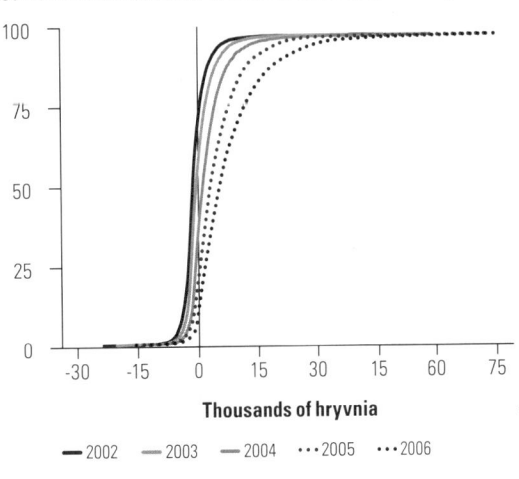

Thousands of hryvnia

— 2002 — 2003 — 2004 ··· 2005 ··· 2006

Source: Staff calculations.
Note: Financial margin is calculated as $M_i = DI_i - BLC_i - DSE_i$ where I = household; M_i = margin of the i'th household; DI_i = disposable income of the i'th household; BLC_i = basic living costs (defined by country) of the i'th household; and DSE_i = debt service expenditure of the i'th household, as explained in the main text. BLC (basic living costs) is based on the subsistence-level budget/expenditure in Belarus, Kazakhstan, and Ukraine, and on the national poverty line in Serbia.

1. Based on subsistence-level budget.
2. Based on subsistence level.
3. Quarterly data are analyzed.
4. Based on poverty line of $5.00/person/day in 2005 price.
5. Based on subsistence level of average expenditure.

References

Alam, A., S. Kathuria, and O. Vybornaia, 2008a, "Rising Food Grains and Energy Prices in ECA: Some Economic and Poverty Implications, and Policy Responses," mimeo, World Bank.

Alam, A., S. Kathuria, and O. Vybornaia, 2008b, "Food Grains and Energy Prices in ECA: An Update," mimeo, World Bank.

Alam, Asad, and Victor Sulla, 2009, "An Update on Income Poverty and Inequality in Eastern Europe and the Former Soviet Union," mimeo (Washington, DC: The World Bank).

Alderman, Harold, and Christina H. Paxson, 1992, "Do the Poor Insure? A Synthesis of the Literature on Risk and Consumption in Developing Countries," World Bank Policy Research Working Paper No. 1008 (Washington, DC: The World Bank).

Beer, Christian, and Martin Schurz, 2007, "Characteristics of Household Debt in Austria: Does Household Debt Pose a Threat to Financial Stability?" *Monetary Policy and the Economy*, 2nd Quarter: pp. 58–79.

Bekaert, Geert, Campbell R. Harvey, and Christian Lundblad, 2006, "Growth Volatility and Financial Liberalization," *Journal of International Money and Finance*, Vol. 25 (3): pp. 370–403.

Brownbridge, Martin, and Sudharshan Canagarajah, 2009, "How Should Fiscal Policy Respond to the Economic Crisis in the Low Income Commonwealth of Independent States? Some Pointers from Tajikistan," World Bank Policy Research Working Paper No. 4970 (Washington, DC: The World Bank).

Calvo, Guillermo, Alejandro Izquierdo, and Ernesto Talvi, 2006a, "Phoenix Miracles in Emerging Markets: Recovering without Credit from Systemic Financial Crises," NBER Working Paper No. 12101 (Cambridge, Great Britain, National Bureau of Economic Research).

———, 2006b, "Sudden Stops and Phoenix Miracles in Emerging Markets," *American Economic Review*, Vol. 96 (2): pp. 405–410.

Campbell, John Y., and Joao F. Cocco, 2007, "How Do House Prices Affect Consumption? Evidence from Micro Data," *Journal of Monetary Economics*, Vol. 54 (3): pp. 591–621.

Central Bank of the Russian Federation, 2008, *Banking Supervision Report 2007* (Moscow: Central Bank of the Russian Federation).

Chen, Kechen, and Mali Chivakul, 2008, "What Drives Household Borrowing and Credit Constraints? Evidence from Bosnia and Herzegovina," IMF Working Paper No.

08/202 (Washington, DC: International Monetary Fund).

Coady, David, and others, 2006, "The Magnitude and Distribution of Fuel Subsidies: Evidence from Bolivia, Ghana, Jordan, Mali, and Sri Lanka," IMF Working Paper No. 06/247 (Washington, DC: International Monetary Fund).

de Koning, Jaap, Mariana Kotzeva, and Stoyan Tzvetkov, 2007, "Mid-Term Evaluation of the Bulgarian Programme 'From Social Assistance to Employment,'" in Jaap de Koning, ed., *Employment and Training Policies in Central and Eastern Europe* (Amsterdam: Dutch University Press).

Dudwick, Nora, Elizabeth Gomart, and Alexandre Marc, with Kathleen Kuehnast, 2003. *When Things Fall Apart: Qualitative Studies of Poverty in the Former Soviet Union* (Washington, DC: World Bank).

European Central Bank (ECB), 2009, *Financial Stability Review*, June (Frankfurt: European Central Bank).

_____, 2007, *EU Banking Sector Stability*, November (Frankfurt: European Central Bank).

Fankhauser, Samuel, Yulia Rodionova, and Elisabetta Falcetti, 2008, "Utility Payments in Ukraine: Affordability, Subsidies and Arrears," *Energy Policy*, Vol. 36 (11): pp. 4168–4177.

Freund, Caroline L., and Christine Wallich, 1997, "Public Sector Price Reforms in Transition Economies Who Gains? Who Loses? The Case of Household Energy Prices in Poland," *Economic Development and Cultural Change*, Vol. 46 (1): pp. 35–59.

Ghosh, Atish R., Marcos Chamon, Christopher Crowe, Jun I. Kim, and Jonathan D. Ostry, 2009, "Coping with the Crisis: Policy Options for Emerging Market Countries," IMF Staff Position Note No. SPN/09/08 (Washington, DC: International Monetary Fund).

Gupta, Sanjeev, Marijn Verhoeven, Robert Gillingham, and others, 2000, *Equity and Efficiency in the Reform of Price Subsidies: A Guide for Policymakers* (Washington, DC: International Monetary Fund).

Habermeier, Karl, İnci Ötker-Robe, Luis Jacome, Alessandro Giustiniani, Kotaro Ishi, David Vávra, Turgut Kışınbay, and Francisco Vazquez, 2009, "Inflation Pressures and Monetary Policy Options in Emerging and Developing Countries: A Cross Regional Perspective," IMF Working Paper No. 09/1 (Washington, DC: International Monetary Fund).

Holló, Dániel, 2007, "Household Indebtedness and Financial Stability: Reasons to Be Afraid?" *MNB Bulletin*, November (Budapest: National Bank of Hungary).

International Monetary Fund (IMF), 2009a, *World Economic Outlook*, April (Washington, DC: International Monetary Fund).

_____, 2009c, *Europe Regional Economic Outlook*, April (Washington, DC: International Monetary Fund).

_____, 2009d, *Global Financial Stability Report*, April (Washington, DC: International Monetary Fund).

_____, 2009e, "Republic of Latvia: Request for Stand-By Arrangement—Staff Report; Staff Supplement; Press Release on the Executive Board Discussion; and Statement by the Executive Director for the Republic of Latvia" (Washington, DC: International Monetary Fund).

_____, 2008a, *World Economic Outlook*, October (Washington, DC: International Monetary Fund).

_____, 2008b, *World Economic Outlook*, April (Washington, DC: International Monetary Fund).

_____, 2008c, "Food and Fuel Prices—Recent Developments, Macroeconomic Impact, and Policy Responses," June 19 (Washington, DC: International Monetary Fund).

_____, 2006b, "Household Credit Growth in Emerging Market Countries," *Global Financial Stability Report*, September, Chapter II.

Johansson, Martin W., and Mattias Persson, 2006, "Swedish Households' Indebtedness and Ability to Pay: A Household Level Study," *Sveriges Riksbank Economic Review*, No. 3: pp. 24–40.

Kang, S. J., and Y. Sawada, 2008, "Credit Crunch and Household Welfare: The Korean Financial Crisis," *Japanese Economic Review*, Vol. 59 (4): pp. 438–458.

Karasulu, Meral, 2008, "Stress Testing Household Debt in Korea," IMF Working Paper No. 08/255 (Washington, DC: International Monetary Fund).

Kluve, Jochen, Hartmut Lehmann, and Christoph M. Schmidt, 1999, "Active Labor Market Policies in Poland: Human Capital Enhancement, Stigmatization, or Benefit Churning?" *Journal of Comparative Economics*, Vol. 27 (1) (March): pp. 61–89.

Kose, M. Ayhan, Eswar Prasad, and Marco E. Terrones, 2003, "Financial Integration and

Macroeconomic Volatility," *IMF Staff Papers*, Vol. 50, Special Issue: pp. 119–142.

Laeven, Luc, and Thomas Laryea, 2009, "Principles of Household Debt Restructuring," IMF Staff Position Note No. SPN/09/15 (Washington, DC: International Monetary Fund).

Lampietti, Julian, and others, 2007, *People and Power: Electricity Sector Reforms and the Poor in Europe and Central Asia* (Washington, DC: The World Bank).

_____, ed., 2004, "Power's Promise: Electricity Reforms in Eastern Europe and Central Asia," Working Paper No. 40 (Washington, DC: The World Bank).

Lubyova, Martina, and Jan C. van Ours, 1999, "Effects of Active Labor Market Programs on the Transition Rate from Unemployment into Regular Jobs in the Slovak Republic," *Journal of Comparative Economics*, Vol. 27 (1): pp. 90–112.

May, Orla, and Merxe Tudela, 2005, "When Is Mortgage Indebtedness a Financial Burden to British Households? A Dynamic Probit Approach," Bank of England Working Paper No. 277 (London: Bank of England).

National Bank of Serbia (NBS), 2008, "2007 Financial Stability Report" (Belgrade: National Bank of Serbia).

Rosenberg, Christoph B., and Marcel Tirpák, 2008, "Determinants of Foreign Currency Borrowing in the New Member States of the EU," IMF Working Paper No. 08/173 (Washington, DC: International Monetary Fund).

Sawada, Y., K. Nawata, M. Ii, and J. Lee, 2007, "Did the Credit Crunch in Japan Affect Household Welfare? An Augmented Euler Equation Approach Using Type 5 Tobit Model," CIRJE Discussion Papers F-Series No. 498 (Tokyo: University of Tokyo).

U.S. Bureau of Labor Statistics, 1997, "The Experimental CPI Using Geometric Means (CPI-U-XG)" (Washington, DC: U.S. Bureau of Labor Statistics).

Vatne, Bjørn Helge, 2006, "How Large Are the Financial Margins of Norwegian Households? An Analysis of Micro Data for the Period 1987–2004," *Norges Bank Economic Bulletin*, December 2006, Vol. LXXVII (4): pp. 173–180.

Vodopivec, Milan, 1999, "Does the Slovenian Public Work Program Increase Participants' Chances to Find a Job?" *Journal of Comparative Economics*, Vol. 27 (1) (March): pp. 113–130.

von Braun, Joachim, 2008, "The Food Crisis Isn't Over," *Nature*, 456 (11): p. 701.

World Bank, 2009a, "The Expected Impact of the Global Financial Crisis on the World's Poorest," mimeo (Washington, DC: The World Bank). A note prepared by the World Bank's Development Economics Vice Presidency in February 2009.

_____, 2009c, "Tajikistan: Poverty Assessment" (Washington, DC: The World Bank).

_____, 2009d, "Armenia: Implications of the Global Financial Crisis for Poverty," Report No. 47770-AM (Washington, DC: The World Bank).

_____, 2009e, "Bulgaria: Poverty Implications of the Global Financial Crisis for Poverty" (Washington, DC: The World Bank).

_____, 2009f, "Protecting Core Public Spending during the Global Economic Crisis," Briefing Note prepared by the World Bank's PREM Vice Presidency.

_____, 2009g, *Russian Economic Report No. 18* (Washington, DC: The World Bank).

_____, 2009h, "Social Protection and Economic Shocks in ECA: The 'Social Side' of the Global Crisis," Social Protection Team (Washington, DC: The World Bank).

_____, 2009j, "In Focus: Domestic Credit Developments," EU10 Regular Economic Report, February (Washington, DC: The World Bank).

_____, 2008a, "Rising Food Prices: Policy Options and World Bank Response," Background.

_____, 2008b, "PREM Guidance Note on the Financial Crisis" (Washington, DC: The World Bank).

_____, 2005, *Growth, Poverty, and Inequality: Eastern Europe and the Former Soviet Union* (Washington, DC: The World Bank).

_____, 2004, "Growth, Employment, and Living Standards in Pre-Accession Poland," Report No. 30078 (Washington, DC: The World Bank).

Zezza A., B. Davis, C. Azzarri, K. Covarrubias, L. Tasciotti, and G. Anriquez. 2008, "The Impact of Rising Food Prices on the Poor," ESA Working Paper, 08-07 (Rome: FAO).

Żochowski, D., and S. Zajączkowski, 2008, "Stress Testing Household Indebtedness: Impact of financial vs. Labor market shocks," World Bank Workshop, Macro Risks and Micro Responses.

_____, 2007, "The Distribution and Dispersion of Debt Burden Ratios among Households in Poland and Its Implications for Financial Stability," IFC Bulletin No. 26 (Basel: BIS).

Notes

1. For a discussion of the origins of these shocks and their global implications, see, for example, IMF WEO (October 2008a, 2009a), IMF Global Financial Stability Report (October 2008, April 2009) and, for a particular focus on commodity price movements, see the World Bank Global Economic Prospects (2009).
2. See also World Bank (2009j).
3. See OECD (2006).
4. See also World Bank (2004 and 2005). More formally, the (total) elasticity of the poverty headcount with respect to growth in average per capita consumption has been about –1.3 in these countries, compared with –3.4 in the middle-income CIS countries.
5. See Calvo, Izquierdo, and Talvi (2006a and 2006b). Among the ECA countries in their sample are the Russian Federation, Slovenia, and Ukraine.
6. See also IMF (2009a).
7. See Ghosh et al. (2009).
8. IMF (2008b, 2008c).
9. "Rising Food Prices Hit Eastern Europe," *The Wall Street Journal*, March 12, 2009.
10. Fankhauser et al. (2008). Under the ongoing IMF-supported program, energy tariff increases in Ukraine are expected to be phased-in (IMF, 2009c).
11. Von Braun (2008).
12. Campbell and Cocco (2007).
13. This and the next paragraphs draw heavily from World Bank (2009h).
14. This section draws heavily from the work of Alam and Sulla (2009). Their analysis is based on the same internationally comparable consumption aggregates and poverty and vulnerability lines used in this chapter.
15. Central Bank of the Russian Federation (2008).
16. This problem has been modeled as a problem of inter-temporal consumption smoothing under a stochastic income process. Using this framework, some papers (Kang and Sawada, 2008; Sawada, Nawata, Ii, and Lee, 2007) estimate the welfare costs of a credit crunch. For example, over the period of the Korean "twin" crises of 1997–1998, the marginal utility loss due to the credit crunch was found to be higher among lower-income households, ranging from 29.3 percent for the bottom quartile to 14.2 percent for the richest quartile. In Japan in 1998, the marginal utility loss ranged from 10.3 to 2.4 percent for the bottom and top income quartiles, respectively.
17. Rosenberg and Tirpák (2008) suggest that EU membership promotes borrowing in foreign currency *indirectly*, such as through capital account liberalization that then facilitates access to foreign funds. In addition, they also observe that EU membership seems associated with greater private

sector confidence in the stability of the exchange rate and the eventual adoption of the euro.

18. National Bank of Serbia (2008).

19. See Rosenberg and Tirpák (2008) for a brief survey of some of these policies. But the results of their analysis suggest that the observed cross-country differences are in large part explained by interest rate differentials.

20. Campbell and Cocco (2007).

21. Żochowski and Zajączkowski (2007 and 2008).

22. See, for example, the discussions on Latvia summarized in IMF (2009e).

23. See, for example, Holló (2007), Żochowski and Zajączkowski (2008), Johansson and Persson (2006), and others.

24. The financial margin is calculated as $M_i = DI_i - BLC_i - DSE_i$ where i = household; M_i = margin of the i'th household; DI_i = disposable income of the i'th household; BLC_i = basic living costs (defined by country) of the i'th household; and DSE_i = debt service expenditure of the i'th household. See also Johansson and Persson (2006) and Vatne (2006). Nationally defined minimum consumption expenditures, minimum consumption baskets, or poverty lines have been typically used to proxy basic living expenses.

25. See May and Tudela (2005) on how this threshold interest payment level is determined. It may be argued that a 20 percent threshold seems overly restrictive because other stress testing exercises have used a 30 percent threshold instead (e.g., Beer and Schurz, 2007; ECB, 2007; Karasulu, 2008). However, those exercises were based on comprehensive data on household debt (including mortgage debt, consumer loans, and other household debt) and household debt service (covering both interest payments and principal repayments). In the case of SILC data, we have information on mortgage interest payments, thus requiring the relevant interest payment threshold. Nonetheless, we also use a 30 percent threshold as a sensitivity test.

26. This refers to the analysis of EU-SILC data, which are for 2007, and thus the two-year period for these EU countries captures the recorded *increase* in unemployment rates between 2007 and 2009. In the case of HBS data, which are for CIS and other countries and refer to older years (e.g., 2006), we use a longer time horizon (e.g., 5-year period) to capture historical *increases* (rather than decreases) in unemployment rates.

27. The procedure is carried out in Stata using the *r binomial* routine.

28. It is assumed that the ratio of unemployment rates within each subgroup is constant before and after the unemployment shock. For example, if the rural unemployment rate is double that of urban unemployment, the ratio is kept constant after the new "unemployed" are selected.

29. Neither can we estimate a probability model for taking on loans with variable interest rate, as the relevant information does not exist in the household survey.

30. Holló (2007), for example, simulates a 5 percentage point interest rate shock in Hungary.

31. It should be pointed out that only those who were previously employed are subjected to the shock. Unemployed individuals as well as unpaid family workers and agricultural workers and farmers producing for their own consumption are excluded.

32. At the time these stress tests were conduct, the study team was unaware of publicly available aggregate data on the share of household loans with variable interest rates.

33. See, for example, Beer and Schurz (2007).

34. See, for example, OECD (2006) and ECB (2009).

35. IMF (2008a).

36. Coady et al. (2006).

37. Coady et al. (2006).

38. There are of course offsetting developments that are difficult to quantify in net terms. Rising oil prices through late 2008 bolstered the GDP growth of oil-exporting countries such as Russia to about 7.3 percent on average in 2007. In turn, the growing demand from the region's oil-exporting countries has increased exports among smaller oil-importing countries.

39. This was previously noted in World Bank (2005) as well. See the report's data and methodology appendix.

40. Baclajanschi et al. (2007).

41. Alam et al. (2008a and 2008b).

42. See, e.g., Baclajanschi et al. (2007); Freund and Wallich (1997); and Coady et al. (2006).

43. The Laspeyres index is also known as an arithmetic mean index, calculated as the sum of weighted prices in time t+1, retaining base period consumption shares. The second is a geometric index of relative price change (RG) using the base period consumption shares as weights: $RG = \prod (P_{t+1,i} / P_{t,i}) W_{t,i}$ where $P_{t+1,i}$ and $P_{t,i}$ are the prices of the i'th consumption items in the new and base time periods, respectively, and $W_{t,i}$ is the share of the i'th consumption item in total consumption. See also Pollak (1989), Gupta et al. (2000), U.S. Bureau of Labor Statistics (1997), and the Technical Appendix in Baclajanschi et al. (2006).

44. This is based on Sarosh Sattar's unpublished work and data, which she generously shared. Any errors of interpretation are the study team's own.

45. Zezza et al. (2008). The data were generously provided by the authors.
46. See, for example, World Bank (2009a and 2005).
47. Ideally, private consumption growth projections from the Global Economic Prospects database would have been preferable. However, country-level projections were not readily available. The calculations in World Bank (2009a) are based on the Global Economic Prospects database.
48. See also Alam and Sulla (2009).
49. World Bank (2005).
50. This section draws in part from the caveats outlined in World Bank (2009a).
51. This and other references throughout the report to the welfare costs of previous crisis in ECA are drawn from the comprehensive review of the literature conducted by Victoria Levin.
52. In fact, there are two underlying assumptions: (i) the first concerns the relationship between GDP growth and average per capita consumption and (ii) the second concerns the relationship between the growth in average per capita private consumption as measured in national accounts and the growth in per capita household consumption as measured in household surveys. The first (i) is estimated as explained in the data section and the second (ii) assumes a full pass-through. As discussed in World Bank (2009a), the poverty impact may be overstated if the actual fall in household consumption is less than the fall in national accounts-based private consumption.
53. See, for example, Bekaert, Harvey, and Lundblad (2006).
54. See, for example, Kose, Prasad, and Terrones (2003). In fact, up to a certain threshold, relative consumption volatility may *rise* with greater financial intermediation.
55. IMF (2009a).
56. See also Dudwick et al. (2003).
57. This is based on the estimated total ECA population of about 477 million, using UN population data.
58. World Bank (2005). See Table 2.1.
59. World Bank (2009c).
60. World Bank (2009d).
61. World Bank (2009e).
62. World Bank (2009g).
63. Alderman and Paxson (1992).
64. The full set of references is available on request.
65. See World Bank (2008b) for a more comprehensive discussion.
66. World Bank (2009f). The calculations are based on the April 2009 WEO and are consistent with other WEO-based calculations elsewhere in this report.
67. See, for example, Brownbridge and Canagarajah (2009).
68. This and subsequent paragraphs are drawn heavily from World Bank (2009h). The report provides an excellent, comprehensive review of the region's social protection system.
69. According to a recent report (World Bank 2008b), Turkey initiated a CCT program during the 2001 crisis and the program has been found to be effective. FYR Macedonia is now in the process of developing a CCT, with a special focus on youth and infants.
70. We thank Sophie Sirtaine for raising these points.
71. See Laeven and Laryea (2009).
72. If financial assistance is provided only to the households in the lowest quintile, the cost of providing assistance is of course substantially smaller.
73. For a detailed discussion of these issues, see Alam et al. (2008a and 2008b).
74. See Lampietti et al. (2007) and Lampietti (2004) for a more comprehensive discussion.
75. The region's experience with workfare may be broader than these four evaluations may suggest. For example, during the 1998–2000 period, participation rates (as percentage of registered unemployed) in public works were about 15 percent in Bulgaria, 11 percent in Estonia, 27 percent in Hungary, 19 percent in Russia, 3.2 percent in Slovakia, 2.2 percent in Poland, and 11.6 percent in Ukraine. Unfortunately, this rich experience has not been evaluated.
76. De Koning, Kotzeva, and Tzvetkov (2005).
77. Lubyova and van Ours (1999).
78. M. Vodopivec (1999).
79. J. Kluve, H. Lehmann, and C. M. Schmidt (1999).
80. IMF (2006b).
81. Rosenberg and Tirpák (2008).